MORE POWER TO YOUR SKATING

MORE POWER

TO YOUR SKATING

A COMPLETE TRAINING PROGRAM
FOR ICE HOCKEY PLAYERS OF ALL AGES

Barbara Williams

Shirley Walton Fischler

MACMILLAN PUBLISHING CO., INC.
NEW YORK

Macmillan Publishing Co., Inc.
866 Third Avenue, New York, N.Y. 10022
Collier Macmillan Canada Ltd.

Library of Congress Cataloging in Publication Data
Williams, Barbara.
More power to your skating.
1. Hockey. I. Fischler, Shirley, joint author.
II. Title.
GV847.W64   796.9′62   79–20366
ISBN 0–02–629040–5

First Printing 1979

Printed in the United States of America

Linda Rosenbaum was the head photographer unless otherwise noted.

Design by Shaun Johnston

Cover photo: Skating coach Barbara Williams with New York Islander
defenseman Dave Lewis and his son, Ryan Patrick.

Song on page 171 copyright © 1979 by Teddy and Robert Rondinelli.

To my three wonderful children, Randy, Tommy, and Cyndee, whom I love very much. I am most grateful for the patience they have shown while putting up with Mom's nerves over the last year.

Barbara Williams
Kings Park, New York
April, 1979

To all the women who approached me wishing to be hockey players or hockey writers. And, of course, to Stan, Ben, and Simon, who always add more power to my life.

Shirley Walton Fischler
Manhattan
April, 1979

CONTENTS

PREFACE:

ABOUT BARBARA WILLIAMS

I was born in Brooklyn, New York, and raised on Long Island—not Canada, as so many people I've taught have assumed. In some ways my background on ice is similar to that of the average professional hockey player: I laced on my first pair of skates at the tender age of five, and I spent a great portion of my childhood working very hard at my sport. I even won some medals and ribbons, and I turned professional at the age of twenty-two.

I will never forget the day when, at the age of five, I walked into a park with my mom and saw a woman figure skater on a pond. I was awed by her beautiful, graceful moves, and I said to Mom, "I am going to be just like that lady."

Later that day I saw a movie on TV called the "Countess of Monte Cristo" starring Sonja Henie. Watching this former Olympic star who popularized figure skating absolutely clinched my dream. Little did

I know that a few years later I would be coached by Howard Nicholson, Henie's former coach.

Before Howard, though, Vera Cross was my coach. She was a gentle, warm, and very giving person—almost the antithesis of Nicholson, who was very strict and disciplined; I think I'm still a little afraid of him! These two opposite personalities had a profound influence on my career, both as skater and as coach.

I first taught under the directorship of James Tester, then head of the Nassau County Skating School in Manhasset. It was Jimmy who taught me the art of teaching larger groups as though I were teaching only one person. This quality helped enormously when I began teaching power skating classes with 40 boys.

Patricia Walcot, Director of Racquet & Rink on Long Island, gave me my truly big break. She had hired me as her assistant in the figure skating school, but one day she asked if I would teach some young hockey players how to skate. That was the day I stood and watched my first "kid hockey" game, and noted how horribly the youngsters skated. From there I went on to a goalie clinic with Islander goalies Billy Smith and Glenn "Chico" Resch, and then finally I became skating coach for the team.

The first day I skated out to coach the Islander team, I wanted nothing more than to skate right off the rink and never come back—I was convinced they were never going to accept me, a small, rather powerless looking female. But after a few nervous minutes, we proceeded as though it were just another session. And my relationship with those professionals—and their coach, Al Arbour—was simply wonderful, the whole time.

That's not to say that I haven't had my share of "weird" and bizarre episodes resulting from my being a woman in a man's sport. Some of these stories I would like to share with you. Shortly after I began coaching the Islanders, two elderly women watching a session called me over and asked if I could resolve a dispute they were having. I figured they had a question about technique or some such thing and was hardly prepared for the question: "What number are you on the team— number two or eight?"

I was crushed, but then realized it was really a compliment to my professionalism to be taken for a professional hockey player.

I remember the day Gary Howatt's wife had their first baby, Brody. Being the proud father, Gary passed cigars out to everyone, including me. Later when I went up to the snack bar for tea, I laid the cigar on the counter, at which point a gentleman standing next to me said, "Why, isn't that funny, we smoke the same brand!"

And how could I ever forget what happened when I was an instructor at a hockey seminar for referees. The seminar brochure instructed the pupils to meet "B. Williams" in the locker room before proceeding to the ice. The first thing I saw as I walked into the locker room was a little old man in his jockey shorts and undershirt. I stood there gaping while the poor man almost suffered cardiac arrest on the spot. Hurriedly, I told him I'd meet him on the ice.

When he finally skated on the ice, he came over to me and whispered in my ear, "Gee, I'm real sorry—I thought B. Williams was a guy." Naturally, I make sure now all brochures clearly state BARBARA Williams, so I won't surprise any more half-dressed gentlemen!

One day, wearing my Islander uniform, I went on the ice before the team at the Nassau Coliseum. Suddenly, I heard one of the maintenance men yell to another, "Hey, Harry, they finally did it! The Islanders hired a woman hockey player!" I had a good laugh, but I soon stopped laughing, abruptly.

I am in the habit, when teaching a hockey skating class, of pushing the goalie cages back against the boards, and I had done so this day. I started the class by skating backward, with the players skating toward me, when the next thing I knew I was sitting on my behind *in* one of the goals. Apparently one of the maintenance men had decided to work on the boards that day, and had moved one of the goalie nets back onto the ice. Somewhat stunned, I stood up quickly, promptly cracking my head on the crossbar, at which point Gary Howatt started calling for the trainer. Ron Waske came over and told me to go home and put ice on what was a rapidly growing goose egg, and to top off the day, Bert Marshall skated over and said quietly, "I never saw a blonde score a goal before—when *she* was the goal!"

Then there was the Christmas when my college power skating class left me some beautifully wrapped gifts, which I thought was so considerate. I opened them: a box of "Old Spice on a Rope," followed by Mennen aftershave lotion, a striped tie—and what woman's Christmas would be complete without a pink jock strap! I didn't know whether to laugh or cry.

Some days I could take the ribbing and laugh at it, but other times it hurt—I felt my identity as a woman was being submerged. I guess that's why I wore a dress to nearly every Islander home game; naturally, none of the players recognized me!

Basically, however, the whole experience has been worth almost every minute, and the difficult moments have simply required a sense of humor. I am now happily committed to spreading the word about power skating; I feel it's an increasingly important part of hockey skills for children as well as for pros.

ACKNOWLEDGMENTS

To the New York Islanders coach—Al Arbour—for giving me the opportunity to work with your team and the confidence that you had in me.

General Manager—Mr. Bill Torrey—for naming me the "First Woman Skating Coach in the National Hockey League." Thank you.

Secretary—Jill Knee—for being there when I needed a friend.

To all the Islander Players—Thanks for all your valuable quotes for my book and it has been the greatest experience in my life to have worked with such a bunch of wonderful guys.

To Dave Lewis and son Ryan Patrick for shooting the cover of my book.

Ice Time—H. C. Butler, Manager, Racquet & Rink, Farmingdale, New York
        Bob Ahrens, Manager, Superior Ice Rink, Kings Park, New York
Equipment—Northland Sticks, Stan Mikita Helmets, Minnesota
Sports Shop—Racquet & Rink Sports Shop, Farmingdale, New York
Artist—Gary Tinschert, Kings Park, New York
Draftsman—Sky Line Detailers, Inc.—Maurice J. Iazzetta, Kings Park, New York
Eye Training—Dr. Leon Revien
Eye Training & Body Building—Mike Revien
"Miss Nimble Fingers" (typing)—Karen Robertson
"A fellow power skating coach" Richie Hiller—Thanks for all your help with the pictures and skating text.

Columbia Pictures—pictures of movie star Robby Benson

Body Building—Neil Dietrichson, Neil's Gym, Saint James, New York

To Peter Burrows and Doreen Schaudel for giving me a sense of humor while writing this book.

To my "little hockey players"—Mark Grabowski, Jimmy Lettis, Kevin Emede, Peter Emede, Christopher Goodrich, David Ramirez, and Matthew Rich.

To my "Warm Up" and "Fault" hockey players—Tommy Giresi, Anthony Salerno, Kevin Rich, Richie Hiller, Jr. and James Lombardi.

To the "Power Skating" Hockey Players—Ali Masters, Larry Chiavaro, Carl Erickson, Howie "Wuz" Gray and our Goalie, Greg Kangesier.

To Norm Ryder—A Fine Hockey Coach—who helped with numerous fine details.

To Mary McGuigan, the "get off the ice" lady—your sense of humor abounds.

To Larry Cangro, "the friendly ape"—thanks for the Senior Men's chapter.

To the gang at "La Femme Fatale," Vinnie, Kathy, Annette, and Susie—thanks for everything.

To "The Three Musketeers"—Lee Tuttle, Nutrition; Bill Hagerty, Physical Fitness; Rigo Predonzan, Off-ice Trainer. Thanks for all your advice and help.

To Nelson—who made me realize how valuable my feet really are!

To Milt Pabst—Thanks for all your expertise on "Equipment Chapter"—Cantiague Park, Hicksville, New York.

To "The Gang," my brothers and sisters—Andrew, Brian, Maureen, Pat, and Michelle. Thanks for all your encouragement and help when I needed it.

To "The Rest of the Gang"—Dick, Debbie, Mike, Steve, Justine, Anthony, and Mark. Thanks for all your enthusiasm.

To my Mom, Chris—Well, I did it!! Thanks for all your love and understanding all these years and your encouragement to finish this book.

To my Dad, Andrew—who gave me the determination and backbone in my life. You will always be with me.

INTRODUCTION

One day in the early 1970s I was in the ice rink teaching several youngsters some figures, when I saw a group of young hockey players having a game in the rink next to ours. The kids were striving mightily, and their parents were cheering them on from the sidelines.

Suddenly I was fascinated. It wasn't the heat of the game, however, which struck me, but the fact that these kids were some of the worst skaters I had ever seen. Yet not one adult there was the least concerned about how Johnny made it down the ice—just as long as he made it, and scored. These youngsters were all in dire need of some very basic skating assistance.

Eureka! Like all great discoveries, the thought that everything I knew and had been teaching for years to figure skaters was applicable to hockey skaters—with slight modifications—suddenly popped into my head, like the proverbial light.

Of course, once I had this realization, I found that I was not alone, which is also typical of "great" discoveries. It wasn't long, however, before I found that precious few people throughout the world were teaching what has come to be called "power skating."

It was the Soviet-NHL hockey series in 1972 which finally brought power skating to the fore. The Russians' incredible, machine-like skating techniques and drills, along with the other superb conditioning processes they've developed almost succeeded in upsetting the complacent NHL players, as they actually did in 1979, during the Challenge Cup.

The NHL has begun to adapt to the startling arrival of the Soviets in their midst, and the concept of power skating has developed and grown in importance. Eventually, the New York Islanders' hockey club recognized the value of skating excellence, and in January, 1977, hired me as the first woman coach in NHL history, through the 1977–78 season. Mind you, I coached skating, not hockey!

The relationship started because I was teaching power skating to youngsters at the Racquet & Rink skating complex in Farmingdale, Long Island, New York, which is also where the Islanders practiced. Islander Bobby Nystrom was my first big league pupil, and several others—including Dave Lewis, Bob Bourne, Jude Drouin, Gerry Hart and Lorne Henning—soon followed suit.

I think that at the beginning Bobby and I were equally amazed at how basic skating techniques—taught at an early age to every figure skater—could make so much difference to hockey skating, but they did and do. After I had begun to teach power skating, I found out about the others who had gone before me, lonely voices far ahead of their time.

Boston Bruins Hall of Famer Eddie Shore, one of the finest defensemen who ever played the game, became known later, when owner of the Springfield Indians minor league team, as a madcap innovator of skating technique. He proposed such way-out tactics (for the time) as teaching ballet to his players to instill more grace and agility.

Shore's controversial concept of the proper stance for a player—knees bent so that the player was in a sort of squat, feet just so many inches apart, and hands two feet apart on the stick—aren't considered at all mad today. In fact, Shore's ideas are quite similar to my own power skating principles.

Then, a few years ago, I came across a now out-of-print volume called *The Hockey Handbook* (A. S. Barnes, 1960) by Lloyd Percival, which contained an entire chapter on the principles of power skating. Percival actually did some training with the Boston Bruins some years ago, but was virtually laughed off the ice at that time. Percival was relegated to obscurity—indeed, I found his book pedantic and difficult to read. However, before his death a few years ago, he must have known that his theories and techniques were being completely vindicated, were even being articulated on the ice by professionals.

Well, then, what *is* power skating?

Reduced to its essentials, power skating is a system for using the edges of one's skate blades, basing all of one's movements on the principles of *inside* and *outside* edging. Along with this simple, but absolutely necessary, concept, there is a basic stance, with the knees bent perhaps more than the average hockey player was once used to, but which, if practiced diligently, gives perfect balance on skates.

One of my favorite surprise tactics with hockey players, who often loom a foot over me (I'm five feet, two inches tall and weigh less than 120 pounds), is to get into my basic stance and then ask them to try to move me. No one has done it yet!

Along with edges and balance, the movement of the shoulders, torso, and hips in coordination with each skate motion, always aware of which edge is to be used for each movement, is the next important element of power skating technique.

Finally, a systematized procession of drills and exercises encompassing all of the basics is a must for proper power skating. Actually, most power skating drills and exercises are variations of exercises which have been used by figure skaters for decades. But until only recently, and particularly after the arrival of those incredibly conditioned Russians, the average hockey player in this country was put on the ice anywhere between five and ten years of age, given some rudimentary skating technique, and as soon as he could stagger the length of the ice, a hockey stick was thrust into his hands.

At the precise moment the youngster acquired that ubiquitous hockey stick, his skating education was basically over except for the standard hockey drills; a perpetual crutch was now his for his career. A surprising number of professional players even today would be virtually lost without that "third leg" to give them added stability. Yet there is hardly a move they make on the ice which they shouldn't be able to execute just as well without that stick.

In addition to the "tripod" approach to skating, how many players have you seen make that funny galloping motion when they want to make a quick start on the ice? I certainly don't want to humiliate any athletes, so I'll omit names, but the number of big league skaters who cannot get started up the ice without churning their legs like a windmill, wasting energy, is depressing. The problem is they have never learned the proper, balanced technique of starting by means of the correct edge. Astounding, isn't it?

Then there is the fellow who is constantly shooting inaccurately from smack in front of the net, or the chap who can't seem to get it past the goalie because he can't execute that "deke" (feint) at the last moment. Why? Because he is doing his turns and crossovers while leading with the wrong shoulder, or shooting with poor balance—all factors based on proper edging.

Power skating will not cure all of a player's problems, nor will it necessarily turn Joe Average into Mr. Superstar. But the simple techniques which I am about to discuss will, without question, give a novice the opportunity to be as fine a player as his or her body and natural talent—combined with good coaching—can give him or her. One thing is sure: a well-schooled body will never betray its possessor as happens all too often with many of today's aspiring hockey stars!

Here we go. (For you older skaters who are eager to get into the meat of power skating, hang on for a bit, because we have to start with some basics for younger power skaters first.)

YOU HAVE TO START
SOMEPLACE

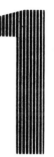

Before we get into power skating with the older young-sters, I want to help parents of children five years old or under—and when I say "under," I truly mean it. It may surprise you, but in fact your child is ready for the ice at the tiny tot stage. A two-year-old can be put on the ice in double runner skates, which is a suggestion many experts would probably dispute. But I say that double runners are definitely fine for the two-year-old for several good reasons.

At this tender age the tot cannot fit into the smallest hockey skate manufactured today (although there are figure skates in tot sizes), so it's double runners by necessity. As if that weren't reason enough, a child this young is unequipped to handle the niceties of balance and technique, posture and movement which are re-quired for the single blade. He or she will feel much more confident on the double runner, while learning the first, most important lesson on ice—*skating is fun.*

Along with these double runners a thin pair of socks under a thicker pair will keep his feet toasty (don't do this with the older child; I'll tell you why later). A well-padded snowsuit is also recommended. No matter how balmy the day or how warm the dressing room, it's chilly on the ice and a snowsuit will be just right. It will serve even better as protection for the child when he or she falls, which tends to happen continuously!

Put a good thick woolen hat *under* the snowsuit hood as added protection against injury when falling. And, of course, don't forget mittens, and pray that the snowsuit is fairly water repellent, since it will be plastered against the ice a great deal of the time. Here is our two-year-old, in Figure 1.

Children at this age often *think* that they don't want to go out in the cold and slog around on ice, just as they usually *think* they don't want to take a bath—then an hour later and after much mopping up, they have to be forcibly removed from the tub. I don't recommend actually forcing a two-year-old to learn how to skate, but usually I've found they really do love it, and with some encouragement take to it quickly. Just be firm and positive and if the protests start, simply state that everyone is going, or some such firm advice.

The most important thing to remember when the two-year-old gets on skates is to see that he or she has a good time. It is not important at this point to stress gliding or keeping the ankles straight. Simply attempt to get the child to "walk" on the ice toward you, remind him to watch where he's going, and help him learn that falling isn't scary.

In fact, once the child learns that falling isn't too bad, you may find that he spends several sessions doing nothing *but* falling down, giggling hysterically all the while. It's a dreadful bore for you, but bear with it—it's the child's way of "conquering" a frightening situation.

The child may also spend most of the time demanding that you pull him around the ice. Again, tolerate it for a while, but encourage independent movement whenever possible. Soon the child will refuse to hold your hand at all, and then you, the parent, will have to stiffen your upper lip and let the little one go it alone.

Figure 1: *"Now, Mark, arms out, like an airplane, on your double runners."*

Impress upon the child that there are rules on the ice rink—everyone skates in one direction (counterclockwise), the middle area is very often reserved for advanced figure skaters, there is no cutting through clumps of skaters, etc. Once the two-year-old gains a bit of confidence, your biggest problem will be dealing with his utter physical abandon on the rink. Tiny novices can be a large menace to older novice skaters who are much more cautious and fearful than the little ones. I remember one little two-year-old who discovered that cutting across the line of "traffic" on the ice produced hilarious results. Bodies would fall all over behind him, or try unsuccessfully to stop as he wildly staggered in front of them. As a good parent/teacher try to maintain a careful balance, encouraging fun and confidence on the one hand, but discouraging wild and reckless behavior on the other. I recommend that you try, if possible, to take the really young skater to morning (preferably weekday rather than weekend) sessions, when the rink will be less crowded.

THREE-YEAR-OLDS

The three-year-old is usually capable of advancing to the single-bladed skate, and I would recommend a figure skate at this point. You may ask why do I recommend a figure skate if the intention is to turn him/her into a hockey player? The answer is simple: because the figure skate has a much higher boot than the hockey skate, and it offers much more support to the child's ankles. More important for your pocketbook, nearly all public ice-skating rinks start renting skates in a child's size 8, but only in figure skates!

The apparel for this age should remain virtually the same as for the two-year-old: a well-padded snowsuit, thick woolen hat under hood, thick mittens or waterproof gloves with lining and *one* good thick pair of socks.

Now you can begin to give your child some easy skating pointers. Always make sure he or she skates to you with head up and arms out to the sides. Ask the child to "walk" to you, this time learning actually to lift his feet off the ice. I find that a little routine is helpful: ask the child to walk four steps (after he or she gets used to lifting the feet) and then glide on both feet, walk four steps, then glide.

Remember that for the child enjoyment and confidence are still (and should be) the two most important objectives at this age; don't make fine distinctions about style. The child will tend to start off by digging in the "toe picks" (the little teeth) on the front of the figure skate blade, but don't worry about it; this can be easily compensated for later on.

One word of caution at this juncture: don't, for heaven's sake, think that you're introducing your child to skating so that you can get some good exercise while at the same time doing something healthy together. You will have to spend a lot of your time completely stationary on the ice, or skating slowly at best. Your main exercise will come in picking up, bending down to instruct, and towing the momentarily lazy little skater! Just make sure that your back and thighs are ready, and call on every reserve of patience you have. Teaching a skill to your child can be one of the most rewarding experiences of parenthood, but you must be willing to commit yourself to expending lots of time, energy, and patience to accomplish it.

FOUR-YEAR-OLDS

The young skater has now been in single-blade figure skates for a year and is ready, at the age of four, to graduate to his/her first pair of hockey skates. The hardest part of this year's education is probably going to be for you, the parent, because I strongly recommend that you take your youngster to a proper skate shop, and have him/her professionally fitted with brand new skates. Just try to feel noble while you shell out the money! After all, when this same child was ready for that important first pair of walking shoes, you went out and bought good quality, well-fitted shoes recommended by a professional shoe salesman, right? Well, you can't do less than the same thing when it comes to hockey skates. I'll explain why it's so important.

First of all, unlike the first pair of shoes which were probably somewhat roomy to allow for growth, hockey skates—or any shoe skate, for that matter—*must* be closely fitted for maximum support to both foot and ankle. Since the hockey skate offers less ankle support than a figure skate, the close fit is doubly important to young ankles.

As I am sure the salesperson will explain, the fit should be so tight that only one pair of socks can be worn underneath. Thus, you must commit yourself to a new pair of skates at least once a year for the rapidly growing child: simply pray that the growth doesn't necessitate two pairs a season!

For the same reasons of proper support and ease of learning, the boot material should be of good quality, while the blade should also be of at least fair quality. If your child is going to wear this skate often and regularly, it would be a waste of your money for lessons and time as parent/coach if the skate material broke down rapidly and failed to give the child proper support and protection. A low-grade, cheap blade will not hold sharpening well, and could cause the child difficulties in learning correct technique.

So, gird your money belt and pay up!

Another hard lesson for you parents will be this recommendation: do not resort to certain "trade in," "swap," or "bargain" deals for your child's skates. Many local rinks and parks will have an assortment of used skates you can purchase for practically nothing, which is very appealing to your pocketbook, but this is the worst thing you can do to your child and his/her feet. Most of these skates offer no support for the ankles and will invariably fit incorrectly.

Sometimes rinks and parks will host "swap" days, where you take your kids' outgrown skates in, find someone with the size you're looking for, and simply trade, or swap, used skates. Obviously, this all too often results in the same lack of support and bad fit as the "bargain" described previously.

The only "trade in" which is worthwhile and beneficial for your child is when a sporting goods outfit applies the value of the used skates toward the purchase price of a new pair. Try to do this, as that first pair cost a pretty penny, so don't simply discard them, but make a point of finding a store which will give you a trade-in price to be applied toward new skates.

Never put your child in someone else's skates, despite the many old stories from hockey players of how they began skating in their big brother's used skates, stuffed with newspapers. That used skate was broken in on someone else's bone structure, and you are simply asking for trouble by forcing your child's bones into the wrong mold. The possible damage and danger to your child's feet and ability would cost you much more than the price of skates in the long run.

Now that we've gotten you parents over the hardest lesson of all, the rest will be relatively painless! The four-year-old should at this time also have a hockey helmet and a pair of hockey gloves. The snowsuit can be discarded at this point for a sweatsuit. Most of the four-year-olds I teach skate in a sweatsuit, which offers flexibility and warmth.

You are now ready to begin gradually teaching your child the basic hockey positions. The first move is to ask him/her to change the arm position from arms out, which is a figure skating technique, to arms at the side, as if holding a stick, closer to the body than in figure skating, shown in Figure 2. Next, he/she should stand with knees slightly bent, but with the head and chest up.

Have the child practice left-together, right-together movements, or step-glide, step-glide. Basically the child is now moving away from walking on the ice, to actually skating. Do *not* talk about "edges" at this point.

The rudiments of a simple snowplow stop can also be taught to the four-year-old. Have the child skate (step-

Figure 2: *a four-year-old in hockey stance.*

Figure 3: *the four-year-old executes the snowplow stop, knees well bent, toes of the skates in slightly.*

Figure 4: *the child has fallen on his softest part—the posterior.*

Figure 5: *he rolls over to get the knees under his body.*

glide, step-glide) toward you down the ice. Once he's moving well, have him glide, with knees well bent. Finally, simply have him put the toes of the skates in slightly and push out to the side with both feet (again, don't talk about edges), as indicated in Figure 3. When the child puts his toes in and pushes to the side, or when you demonstrate this to the child, ask him to do it until he hears a scraping sound on the ice.

This is the same technique used to teach the snow-plow step in downhill skiing, and while the child will actually begin to use the skate edges, explaining this concept usually only causes confusion.

It is important that the four-year-old be taught to fall properly because he/she is not wearing the padding of a snowsuit nor the protection of real equipment. They *must fall on their bottoms*, giving them the greatest protection, and then roll over, get up to their knees and rise, one skate blade at a time, from their knees, as shown in the following sequence (Figs. 4–7).

Figure 6: *Safely on the knees, he prepares to stand.*

Figure 7: *one skate at a time.*

FIVE-YEAR-OLDS

The five-year-old child should now be able to skate down the ice with no problems and with fair confidence. If the child is just beginning to skate at five, though, simply apply the steps and stages we have reviewed for the two to five-year-olds, and within a few weeks he will be able to do this.

The most appealing aspect of skating for the child at this moment (probably) is being outfitted in full hockey regalia for the first time—pads, jersey, garters, helmet, gloves, skates and yes, finally, the stick. Here are two tykes sporting full gear in Figure 8. Kids are eager to learn and are readily teachable at this age, as long as the parent/coach isn't too technical and the elements of fun and pleasure are still maintained. Please, don't scream, don't be too harsh, and don't treat the kid as though the Stanley Cup had to be won next

Figure 8: *NHL—Here we come!*

week—there's time enough later for the youngster to learn the hard facts of hockey life, and he'll be turned off forever if you turn into Simon Legree (or Eddie Shore) at this moment!

While the child is now allowed to have that precious symbol of the game—the stick—in hand, the major emphasis should always be on skating, skating, skating, rather than stick handling or puck carrying, which is too often what today's coaches teach five- and six-year-olds.

Always remember that the child is still learning to skate, while incidentally holding a stick, rather than learning to stick-handle while incidentally being on skates. Skating is the name of the game more than putting that puck in the net; no one will ever get to the net if he can't skate properly!

Some of my fondest and craziest memories are of the first time I began to work with five-year-olds. Some of the incidents were entirely unexpected, as you can see in the following episodes (Figs. 9–11).Since the child

Figure 9: *"Ms. Williams . . . can I go to the little boys' room?" (Photo by Joseph Guerico.)*

Figure 10: *"Who do you think I am . . . Clark Gilles?" (Photo by Joseph F. Guerico.)*

Figure 11: *"Look, Ma, at the 'tomboy'! She has the same skates as my brother." (Photo by Joseph Guerico.)*

Figure 12: *the young skater who leans on his stick has just acquired a "crutch."*

is still mostly involved with skating at this point in his/her development, the first rule to remember is *never let the child lean on the hockey stick*, as the youngster in Figure 12 is so unfortunately demonstrating. Leaning on the hockey stick while skating produces exactly the effect of having a crutch—the child will never learn to distinguish edges properly or balance correctly if allowed to lean on the stick.

Over the years I have found that the best techniques for teaching this age group is the question/answer method on "good hockey position."

"When you are skating down the ice, are you going to have your head up or down?" ("Up.")

"Will your chest be leaning over or up?" ("Up.")

"Will your knees be bent or stiff?" ("Bent.")

"Do we keep our arms up or down?" ("Down.")

"When we skate, do we lift our feet up, or do we keep them low, near the ice?" ("Low, near ice.")

Figure 13: *Barbara is getting a good, loud response from her pupils. (Photo by Joseph Guerico.)*

Make the kids really yell out the answers to these questions, as they practice the "good hockey position." Kids love to holler, as you can see in Figure 13, and the shy, embarrassed ones can sort of yell or not yell while blending into the general clamor. The youngster who doesn't remember the correct response will certainly catch on after hearing the child next to him shriek it out a couple of times!

This is a good place to point out that when a child falls, he/she should *always* get up from a fall to the *knees first*. Never let the child try to jump directly up onto the blades of his skates. Knees first, then up onto the blades one at a time, as this five-year-old demonstrates in Figures 14 and 15.

After a good thorough review of the "good hockey position," it's time, at last, to work on the concept of "edges." This should be done in two stages: *learning* what an edge is, and then *feeling* what an edge is and does.

This moment may become a tough one if the kids

Figure 14: *the five-year-old has just fallen to his knees.*

Figure 15: *to prevent back injury, the child carefully gets back to his feet one skate at a time.*

have not yet learned to distinguish between left and right. It's crucial, but don't laugh, because many children at this age don't know their left from their right and can become hopelessly bollixed up over this seemingly trivial point. There are two simple steps to solve the problem with really young children. First, if the child just can't grasp his/her left from right, put different colored shoe laces on his/her skates—blue for right and red for left, for instance. Naturally, be consistent and don't switch colors on the poor youngster, or he'll be right back where he started—utterly confused.

Second, and even more important, the parent/coach should always demonstrate the drills and exercises with his/her back to the children. Then, when the coach says "right" it will be the same foot as it is for the kids. On the other hand, when I am *explaining* something to the children, I always face them to talk to them.

Now that left and right are, hopefully, straightened out, the child is ready to begin *learning* an edge. First, some simple drills, which are best illustrated by the drawings which follow.

Have the child stand erect (that is, knees still bent slightly in a good hockey position) over his/her skates, then look down at his feet. Now explain, "you're on the *'flats'* of your skates." (Fig. 16)

"Now, press *inside* on your skates." (Fig. 17)

"Then, press *outside* on your skates." (Fig. 18)

This is where good skates will prove their worth. It's simple for a child to relax the ankles inward, which will more or less place the skates on the inside edge of the blade, but the whole idea is to apply *pressure* on the inside edge, too. A good strong skate will not let the child simply relax the ankle, but force him to *press* inside or outside.

Make these exercises into a game; shift from edge to edge asking, "What am I on now?"

Next, have the child "feel" the edge by "piling up snow," while still in a stationary position. And if you look closely at Figure 19, you can see the snow pile.

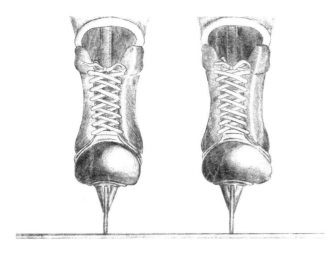

Figure 16: *the "flats" of the blades.*

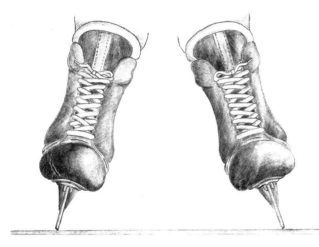

Figure 17: *"Now press inside on your skate."*

Figure 18: *"Now press outside on your skates."*

Figure 19: *the little skater "feels" his inside edge by piling up snow.*

Make the youngster actually *push* his foot out to the side. Then, do right-together, left-together skating steps, this time talking about *inside* edges and really getting them to *push* right-together, left-together.

Now stop and have the kids "pile up snow" again. That simple piling up of snow is the surest sign of really working on an edge and that evidence will also be the quickest way of getting the child to understand what to do.

Note: While the kids will be practicing both edges in a stationary position, as they do this first skating *move* pushing right and then pushing left, they will be skating on their *inside* edges. Check to make sure they apply the pushing pressure with the weight on the ball of the foot and not the toe.

Next, have the children review their previously learned snowplow stop, this time explaining that when they point their toes in, and push, they are using their *inside* edges again. As a practice routine you can have them stand up straight, knees slightly bent, and when you blow the whistle, have them push sideways, toes slightly in, on the *inside* edges.

Figure 20: *balancing on one foot.*

Figure 21: *"Whoops! David, that isn't* quite *balancing on one foot."*

SIMPLE BALANCE DRILL

Have the children skate in a straight line, using the left-together, right-together skating move. Then, as you blow the whistle, have them position and glide, first with the right foot off the ice, then on the next whistle, with the left foot off the ice. Figure 20 shows a little skater balancing, while Figure 21 shows how *not* to do the simple balance drill!

Figure 22: *Barbara and two tykes do the "duck slide."*

Figure 23

Figure 24

It often helps with such exercises to relate them to identifiable hockey figures. Most kids interested in the sport have had a hockey idol for some time, and they love to have what they're doing compared to their stars. For instance, on the balance drill: "When you see Bryan Trottier shoot or take a pass, and do it really well, the reason why is because he has such good balance." Also, be very careful to explain the exercise drills thoroughly before starting them, demonstrating them yourself several times.

DUCK SLIDE

After the simple balance drill the next exercise is the "Duck Slide." (All of these exercises have their counterparts in figure skating, but most hockey players hate to have what they're learning equated with figure skating

Figures 23–26: *the toes point out (FIG. 23), then farther out (FIG. 24), begin to come back in (FIG. 25), and finally the skater is on the "flats" of his skates (FIG. 26).*

Figure 25    Figure 26

Figure 27

Figure 28

terminology.) In the "Duck Slide" the child skates down the ice (always in the basic skating strides of left-together, right-together) and at the whistle signal, he/she squats, stick extended straight out front, head up, and glides along the ice with all weight on the "flats" of the blades, as demonstrated in Figure 22.

FORWARD "SNAKE SQUIGGLES" (INSIDE EDGES)

I tell the children that this exercise gets its name from the fact that their skates will move like snakes down the ice; the pattern they make on the ice should look like snakes. The terms "forward" or "backward" refer to the direction in which the skaters will move. The student should stand up straight, bend knees slightly, and on the whistle, point toes out and press on *inside* edges, then toes in on *inside* edges, then toes straight forward on the "flats" of the blades, as indicated in the following sequence (Figs. 23–26).

Figure 29

Figures 27–29: *the child points the toes in (FIG. 27), presses on inside edges (FIG. 28), then straightens the feet (FIG. 29), ending on the "flats" of the blades.*

BACKWARD "SNAKE SQUIGGLES" (INSIDE EDGES)

Stand up straight, bend knees slightly, on the whistle, point toes in, press on the *inside* edges (Fig. 27), then heels *in* on *inside* edges (Fig. 28), then feet straight on the "flats" of the blades (Fig. 29).

Although the children will practice both inside and outside edges on the stationary drills ("learning" edges, "feeling" edges and stationary snowplow, see pp. 14–18), the moving exercises (forward and backward "squiggles") deal with the *inside* edges only. *Inside* edges are easier for the child to grasp at this age. Skating with the *outside* edges is more complicated to explain, demonstrate, and grasp, and will be treated in the following chapters for older youngsters.

These then, are the basic drills which I teach the five-year-old skater. The basic skating move, simple balance, and edge drills, and the simple snowplow stop are sufficient for the child at this age.

At this point, even if you as parent intend to continue

coaching your child, your child is now old enough and sufficiently capable to be in a professionally coached hockey clinic. I would urge you to take a secondary role now, reinforcing what the child is learning professionally, and especially emphasizing the pleasurable aspects of skating and hockey. It will be better for you and your child if you turn the teaching of the more advanced and disciplined aspects of skating technique over to the professional. This way, you and your child can relax and enjoy each other, while you continue to be supportive.

A word of caution: I have found that American hockey schools for five-year-olds often tend to give a child a stick and a puck and run scrimmages in which putting the puck in the net is the most important aim. The emphasis, however, *should* still be on skating, so research the hockey clinic well before you enroll your child in it. Make sure that basic power skating techniques are *at least* as important as hockey skills and drills, if not more so.

Unfortunately, I also often find parents enrolling children in five-year-old hockey clinics when the children can't really skate. The coach more often than not will simply resort to bringing chairs out on the ice and having the child push the chairs around in order to "learn skating" as we see in Figure 30. This is nothing but a crutch and will never teach real skating. Don't waste your money on an expensive hockey clinic if your child can't skate—hire someone to teach him/her skating *first*, if you can't do it yourself.

It's true that children in Canada are often *not* taught how to skate properly, but learn how to skate anyway, because they're virtually "born" on the ice. They have easy access to lots of ice time at a relatively cheap price. This is not possible in the United States where there is less ice and ice time is more expensive. Therefore, in this country, we have to concentrate on learning good skating in limited time. Believe me, it's useless to skip this fundamental stage.

Figure 30: *pushing a chair on the ice is* no *way to learn skating.*

Experts in early childhood development have determined that it is important for the overall development of the child to go through every stage of physical development; i.e., the baby first "rocks," then crawls, then stands, then walks. The child who skips crawling and jumps right to walking, while precocious as a baby, may develop physiological and/or psychological problems because of skipping that important crawling stage. This understanding simply reinforces my advice that you should not expect to create a hockey player out of a child who has never learned to skate properly—it just won't happen!

And don't forget another all-important factor—communication.

Figure 31: *communication among parents, children, and coaches is a must.*

PROPER EQUIPMENT . . . OR BEFORE YOU GET INTO GEAR, BUY THE PROPER GEAR

Now that we've helped both parent and child through the early ages and stages, we're ready to deal with the older skater, and the true development of power skating skills. First, let's talk about the well-dressed, or well-equipped, hockey player.

Earlier I spoke about buying the first pair of hockey skates for the four-or five-year-old, and I said that going to the local department store to buy any old thing with a blade on it was definitely not recommended. Well, this advice applies doubly with the older, more experienced skater.

The way to find the best hockey skate is to find a good sports shop that specializes in the professional fitting of skates. A correctly fitted skate will usually be one or even two sizes smaller than normal shoe size, and will allow only the thinnest sock to be worn inside. A nylon sock is the best, both for warmth and comfort. The boot of the skate should be made of the best quality leather, or it will not give proper support to the ankle *and* will break down rapidly with regular use.

I cannot stress the importance of proper fit strongly enough: there is virtually no such thing as "weak ankles" (*especially* in children), barring some physical abnormality. So, if the skater finds his or her ankles wobbling and sagging constantly, either the skate is a poor one, or the skate's fit is inadequate.

After you've purchased the skates, ask the salesperson in the sporting goods shop to explain the proper way to lace up the skates. Many youngsters—and their parents—think that the tighter the boot is laced, the better the performance, but this is definitely *not* true! In fact, a boot which is too tightly laced will only cut off circulation in the foot and ankle, causing the feet to tire more rapidly and (possibly) initiating foot cramps. The following diagrams (Figs. 32–34) illustrate the dos and don'ts of lacing boots.

Figure 32: *notice the wide spacing of the laces. If laced too loosely, the boot will give no support to the foot and ankle. If the child has a wide foot and the boot is too narrow, this will also occur; make certain of a correct fit. (Drawing by Gary Tinschert.)*

Figure 33: *the laces are chokingly tight, which will cut off the blood's circulation, or if the boot is too wide on a narrow foot, the same will occur. (Drawing by Gary Tinschert.)*

Figure 34: *this is a properly laced skate, not constricted at the top. The lace-ends are not wrapped around the ankles as is so sadly popular with some youngsters. (Drawing by Gary Tinschert.)*

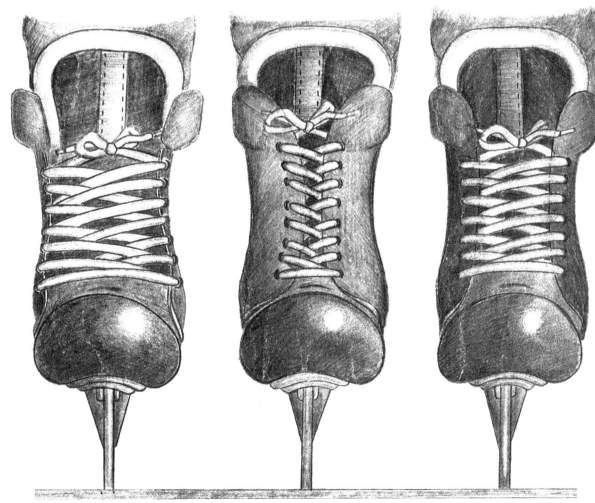

Figure 32   Figure 33   Figure 34

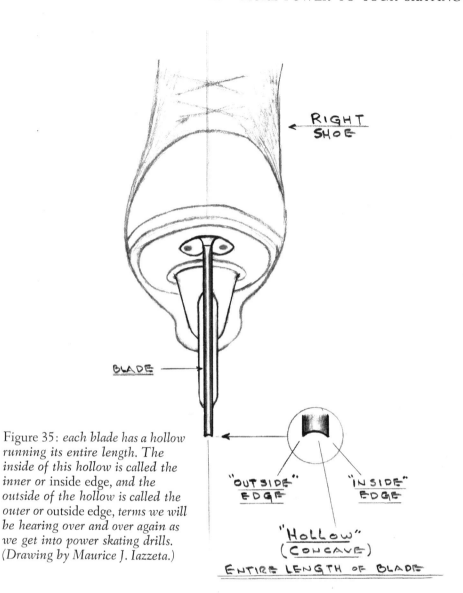

Figure 35: *each blade has a hollow running its entire length. The inside of this hollow is called the* inner *or* inside edge, *and the outside of the hollow is called the* outer *or* outside edge, *terms we will be hearing over and over again as we get into power skating drills. (Drawing by Maurice J. Iazzeta.)*

While you're at it, don't forget to purchase a pair of skate guards, to keep on the blades off-ice, which prolongs the life of the blades by preventing nicks in the metal and by keeping the edges sharp. Don't forget to dry the skate blades after every use (a terry cloth towel is fine), as the blades will rust overnight if placed in the guards wet. Rusty blades make for rough skating and will require constant sharpening.

Understanding the construction of the blade of the skate will ultimately help the child understand how to skate so take a close look at Figure 35. Skate blades should be sharpened regularly—about every two or three weeks—for maximum performance. Dull blades make it almost impossible to skate properly on edges, while correctly sharpened skates will contribute greatly to speed, agility and maneuverability, three absolute essentials to good hockey skating.

As the illustrations point out, many forwards in professional hockey prefer to have their skate blades "rocked" (Fig. 36), while defensemen generally prefer more blade on the ice (Fig. 37). We can't forget the goalie, who must learn to skate the power way, too, but with a blade constructed much differently than that of the other five players on the ice (Fig. 38).

There is a new development in skate blade sharpening which I recommend if you can find a shop which does it and if you're willing to pay a little more for the sharpening. The new method is called "custom radius." It is a system geared to the individual skater and requires sharpening less often (so that the higher expense is almost offset).

A blade profile suitable to the skater's position (forward, defense, goalie), as well as his/her size, weight, and ability is recommended by the professional sharpener. With subsequent sharpenings the settings can be adjusted until the skater finds the blade performing exactly as desired. Then the setting is permanently marked on the blade, ensuring the same blade profile for each new sharpening. This is "custom radius."

Now that the aspiring hockey player has skates and knows how to lace them and sharpen them, we can discuss everything else that is needed for the well-dressed hockey player.

Once again, head for a genuine sporting goods store where the staff knows and understands correct hockey equipment: good equipment is as much a key to good skating and playing as the skate and the stick.

Figure 36: *the typical forward's skate is sharpened into a curve off the ice surface at each end. This curvature is called "rocking" and it enables the forward to turn and take off faster. (Drawing by Gary Tinschert.)*

Figure 37: *defensemen usually prefer more blade touching the ice for greater stability and easier skating backward or stopping. Thus, the blade is straighter, less "rocked" than the forward's. (Drawing by Gary Tinschert.)*

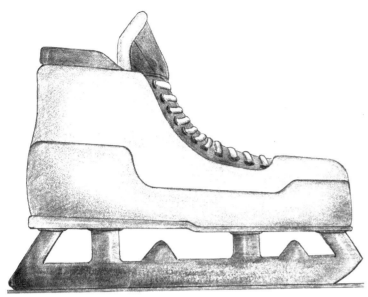

Figure 38: *the goalie's skate blade is very different from the forward's* and *the defenseman's. The blade is almost entirely flat and much thicker. Note that the blade is also "fastened" to the boot in at least four places rather than two, while additional protuberances between blade and boot make it impossible for a puck to pass through if the goalie makes a "skate save."* (*Drawing by Gary Tinschert.*)

First, the helmet. In case the young skater thinks it's unmanly or "unhip" to wear a helmet, he or she had better get rid of this notion pronto because the helmet is *mandatory*. And so, by the way, is the face shield. I can't begin to relate the horrible accidents I've witnessed which never would have occurred had the players been wearing the proper helmet and face shield.

In fact, I think wearing a helmet and face shield should give the player a mental "boost," making him feel more secure, rather than detracting from his feelings of confidence. After all, the puck can move at speeds of more than 100 miles per hour, and the stick can be a terrible weapon on the ice, not to speak of the ice itself, which is nothing if not *hard*.

The helmet is made of strong molded plastic and should offer protection to the ears and temple. The front of the helmet should come all the way down to within one finger's width from the eyebrows and should fit quite snugly. For heaven's sake, don't get a football helmet and expect it to be all right; helmets are made differently for each sport, for very specific reasons, nearly all of which pertain to safety.

Figure 39: *note the snug fit, the helmet coming close to the eyebrows and the face shield. (Photo by Kevin Rich.)*

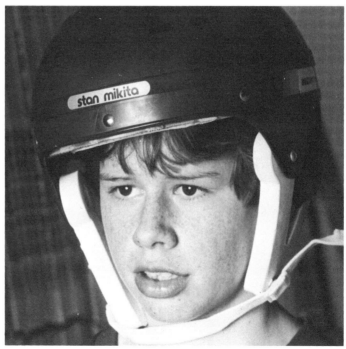

Figure 40: *Tommy's helmet is so large it's lopsided, and it's also without a face mask, which is required in youth hockey. (Photo by Kevin Rich.)*

Figure 39 shows a youngster in a properly fitted helmet and face shield, while Figure 40 shows a child with a poorly fitted helmet. Once again, Dear Parent: Do not buy a helmet for the youngster "to grow into." All this will do is cause accidents when the child skates down ice, because the helmet can slip over his/her eyes. Once the helmet is on the head, there should be very little back and forth "play" or movement.

There are two basic kinds of face masks today: both are made of nylon-coated wire, but one has a plastic shield. Each style comes in two sizes, to fit both youngsters and adults.

Next come the shoulder pads. You can allow for some leeway here for growth, as the straps are adjustable (Fig. 41), but please, don't get them so big that the child is virtually swallowed by the pads—it will simply hinder movement and add an element of annoyance and discomfort.

Figure 41: *properly fitted shoulder pads.*

Elbow pads, genuine hockey gloves and shin guards are next on the required list of equipment, as shown below in Figures 42 through 44.

As for outerwear, well, hockey pants are not very glamorous looking: in fact, they look like bulky Bermuda shorts and give one the general appearance of Yogi Bear! But they offer further protection with built-in hip, kidney, and coccyx (tail bone) padding. They should reach from the top of the knee to the bottom of the ribs, and the waist size should be approximately six inches larger than the skater's actual waist. (Fig. 45). Nylon pants are preferable as they wear the longest.

Figure 42: *elbow pads.*

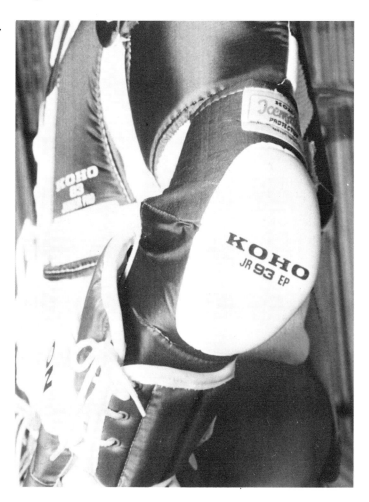

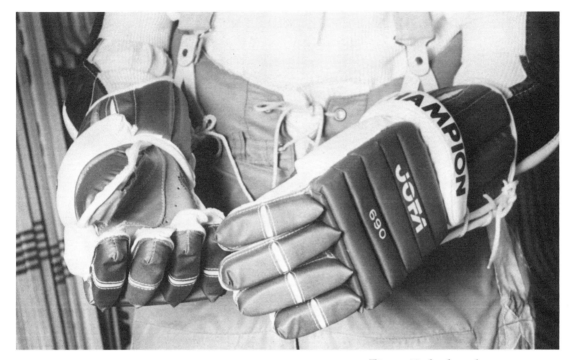

Figure 43: *hockey gloves.*

Figure 44: *shin guards.*

Figure 45: *note that proper hockey pants reach from the top of the knee to the bottom of the rib cage, with a roomy waist.*

Many a tyro hockey player wants to buy a hockey jersey that is nice and snug, thinking that it looks better. It may or may not look "cool," but it certainly will hinder movement. Remember, a lot of bulky gear has to fit under that jersey, and freedom of movement is an absolute necessity in hockey playing. So here is one place where the article of clothing *should* be roomy.

Now, at last, we come to the piece of equipment every would-be hockey player can't wait to purchase— the stick. All sticks may appear to look alike, but nothing could be further from reality, for the stick is a highly personal piece of equipment. Players, after all, come in all heights and shapes; some are left-handed, although most are right-handed. Sticks must vary accordingly.

The first thing to know in choosing a stick is the "lie." The "lie" of the hockey stick is the angle between the ice and the stick when held in the hands in a hockey position. A general rule concerning the correct lie is: stand in a hockey position on the *skates* and hold the stick in one hand with the blade resting on the ice or floor (you will most likely buy your sticks at a store). The bottom of the blade should be flat on the ice. If the toe of the blade is off the ice, pick a lower number lie. If the heel of the blade is off, choose a higher number lie. Most junior sticks for younger players are manufactured with a lie of "6," which is the most popular lie, overall.

As a rule, less experienced players and beginners should use a stick with a high lie (even as much as seven or eight), as this brings the puck closer to the feet, giving young skaters more strength and consequently more power.

Stick length varies from 30 inches to the maximum length of 55 inches. A standard junior hockey stick length for pre-teen youngsters is 48 inches, while the most popular for both teens and adults is 53 inches. A good rule for judging length is to have the butt end of the stick even with the lips when you hold the stick

Figure 46: *a proper tape knob on the stick.*

straight up, while wearing your skates. Mark the point at which it is level with the lips and then cut off the excess.

Be careful, however, for the butt end of the stick can be as dangerous as the blade; so you should tape the butt end with some kind of masking tape to form a knob (Fig. 46). The tape knob will keep the stick from slipping out of the hands as well as protect the player's eyes, teeth, nose and stomach somewhat from a sharp jab of the butt end. You can buy a plastic or rubber safety end if you don't wish to tape the butt.

The blade of the stick should be taped also, to aid in puck-handling by increasing the friction between puck and blade (Fig. 47). Encourage the child to use black tape rather than white, as it will be more visible on the stick and doesn't blend into the ice.

One more essential piece of hockey equipment is a pair of suspenders to hold up the hockey pants, and you also will need a garter belt to hold up the thigh-length professional hockey socks. Don't bother to use Mom's garter belt, because it won't be strong enough to do the job—there are hockey garter belts made just for this purpose.

Miscellaneous necessary equipment includes an athletic supporter and cup (groin injuries are among the most devastating so don't forget to wear them every time you skate), an extra stick, tape roll, a towel, a skate bag, extra laces, a lace tightener, and extra socks.

Once I had a very embarrassing episode concerning hockey equipment. I had just started teaching power skating to older boys—sixteen to eighteen-year-olds in the Met League—and was still unfamiliar with a lot of the standard hockey equipment, especially everything they wore under the jerseys and pants. One night I was training thirty boys: We were skating down ice at high speed when all at once I saw something on the ice. I skated over and picked it up, thinking it was probably one of the small plastic guards that fit into the side pockets of the players' hockey pants. I was a little disturbed, because any hard object on the ice is a potential hazard, so I said in my loudest, most disciplined voice, "Okay, fellas, who owns this?"

There was a complete silence, and after a moment, I repeated myself, even more loudly. Still no response. Then one of the boys' fathers called to me from the stands and I skated over to him. He asked me in a whisper if I knew what I was holding. Getting more irritated by the moment, I muttered something about

Figure 47: *the blade is taped well with black tape for visibility.*

an elbow or knee protector, and he quietly informed me that I was holding an athletic cup. The heat from my red face almost melted the ice under me! As I stood in embarrassment, there was a sudden outburst of laughter from all thirty boys behind me. I could hardly look them in the face, although I admit that I had started to chuckle myself by this time, as I turned and told them to take a few minutes' break in the locker room to figure out who belonged to this piece of "lost equipment!"

After that night I sat down and carefully studied every piece of equipment which is standard hockey gear—inside and outside the jersey and pants!

Well, parents, now that you have equipped your budding hockey skater, I can't say I'd blame you if you have an almost uncontrollable desire to go out and buy a full-sized station wagon! But don't think that lugging all that gear around is going to be sufficient exercise for the youngster, because we've barely begun. Now we're going to talk about getting into shape for the ice!

Figure 48: *"Okay, fellas, who owns this?"*

Figure 49: *Barbara puts her youth hockey skaters through their calisthenic paces. (Photo by Wide World Photos.)*

3

GETTING INTO SHAPE

Between the ages of five and twelve, most children are in naturally good physical condition, largely because they are extremely active. Their muscles aren't really ready to be developed at this stage, but nonetheless, I use calisthenics on the ice for children of this age because it's a good way to teach them discipline and to prepare them for the future—and physically it won't harm them (Fig. 49).

Before we get into diet and exercise, I want to mention to all of you parents that one good way to make sure your youngsters develop their natural inclination toward body movement and vigorous exercise would be for you to limit the time they spend in front of the television set, motionless. I know it can be tough at times, since the TV set has become a national form of "baby-sitting" in this country, but kids spend enough time sitting at school desks, and should be encouraged at other times to be active.

NUTRITION: YOU ARE WHAT YOU EAT!

Since most pre-teen children do tend to get a fair amount of exercise, parents would do well to see that the little ones get sufficient rest and sleep. After that, parents should be most concerned with guiding their children toward a balanced diet, keeping them away, if possible, from our society's tendency to eat "junk" foods and processed foods.

Young people thirteen and older who contemplate a possible career in hockey usually ask for an off-ice training program. At this point I remind them that simply training their bodies will only get them so far if they're not paying attention to what they eat. Nutrition should be a part of any conditioning program.

Most teenagers have heard at some time or another that athletes follow a diet which is very high in protein; protein is the muscle-building part of our diet. Or they have heard that today's professional athletes believe in a high dose of carbohydrates before a game because it gives them quick energy.

As a result of what they've heard about athletes, these youngsters run around stuffing themselves full of red meat and protein supplements, or feasting on platefuls of spaghetti the afternoon of a game. But anyone under the age of twenty-five who is eating in this top-heavy fashion is forgetting one most important thing: the body (or parts of it) is still growing and developing up to the age of twenty-five. Therefore, as a general rule, a balanced diet which includes protein, carbohydrates, and some fats is best for anyone under the age of twenty-five.

I am not a nutritionist, so I do not recommend any hard and fast diet for the youngsters I train. I simply recommend that if they want to try a high protein diet, they include lots of fish and poultry rather than rely on a predominance of red meat. Fish and chicken are high in protein but contain less cholesterol than the red meats. I also point out that certain vegetables, such as soy beans, bear high quantities of protein.

I also point out that carbohydrates are an essential part of a balanced diet, but that we should stay away from carbohydrate in the form of refined sugar. Too many children pop chocolate bars during heavy exercise, on the pretext that it's quick, high energy. Nonsense! The white and yellow vegetables, such as potatoes, cauliflower, and corn are high in natural carbohydrates, as are noodles; and if they simply have to have sugar, they should take it in its natural form in fruits and honey.

I always recommend that athletes take some form of vitamin supplement with minerals included. So many people take vitamins as though they were candy, without thinking about minerals. But growing bodies need large amounts of certain minerals, like calcium and iron.

Last of all, if youngsters insist on a definite diet, or if they have a specific problem with gaining or losing weight, I recommend that they see their family doctor for a controlled diet appropriate to their age and physical development. And for parents besieged by children obsessed with diets and calories, I advise that they go with their children to see the family doctor for good advice, or that they shop with the youngsters for a good book on nutrition.

PHYSICAL CONDITIONING: A LIFETIME HABIT

There are certain basic, unavoidable rules concerning conditioning for athletes. The first basic rule is that someone desiring to be a professional athlete *must* make conditioning a year-round discipline—a lifetime habit, in fact.

The second basic rule about conditioning is that there is no use taking up specific exercises for specific muscles involved in specific sports, without developing overall stamina. And to speak of stamina is to speak first and primarily of exercise which strengthens the heart and lungs.

The forms of exercise which build up the heart, lungs, and general physical endurance and stamina are: running, walking, swimming, bicycling, and jumping rope. They are all excellent, and I can only say that, as with any form of strenuous exercise, they should be done slowly and for short periods of time initially, gradually building up the length of time and speed with which they are done.

I also urge that these endurance activities be performed at alternating speeds and/or rhythms. For instance, while jogging, sprint awhile, then slow down to a trot. When swimming, alternate strokes and the speed of the strokes. Jump rope with alternate feet, then with both feet, etc. By alternating styles and speeds of these endurance or stamina skills, the body is also accustomed to the sudden spurts of energy required by hockey play.

Having initiated a training program for stamina, the athlete is now ready to begin work on developing overall strength. For hockey players, the legs perform the greatest degree of work during play. Running, bicycling, water-skiing and snow-skiing will help build strength in the legs. Skateboarding (done with proper safety gear in designated areas) has become popular with young hockey players, as it builds leg strength, flexibility, and agility (so will surfboarding if you live near a warm ocean!).

Figure 50: New York Islander Richie Hansen is doing a "wrist curl" to strengthen his forearms and wrists. (Photo by Kevin Rich.)

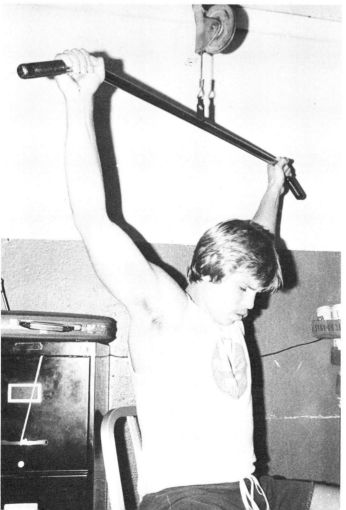

Figure 51: New York Islander Richie Hansen is working on a universal machine doing what is called a "lat-pulldown." He is strengthening his latissimus dorsi muscles (upper back) and also the front part of his upper arm. (Photo by Kevin Rich.)

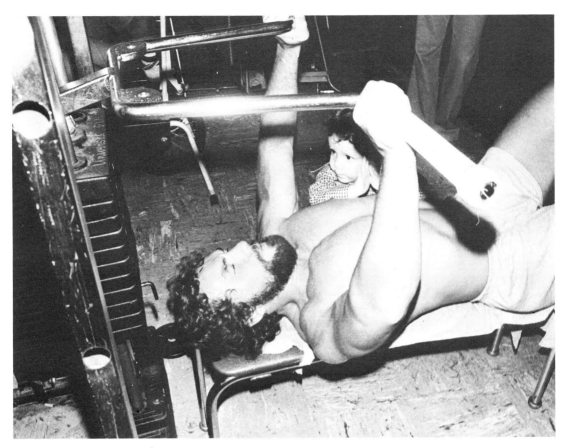

Figure 52: *New York Islander Gary Howatt is working on a universal gym doing a "bench press," which builds chest muscles, triceps, and front deltoids (upper body). Gary's son Brody watches his dad. (Photo by Kevin Rich.)*

Figure 53: *New York Islander Gary Howatt is working on a universal gym doing an "upright row," which will strengthen his trapezius and front deltoid muscles (shoulders). (Photo by Kevin Rich.)*

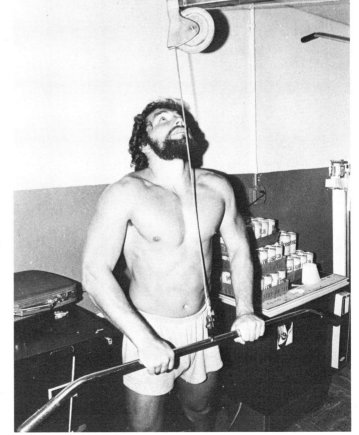

Another sport which is very popular with hockey players and which is directly applicable to hockey is golf. The swing in golf helps to develop similar arm, torso, and eye skills and reflexes. Just remember that unless you *walk* the entire course golf will not do much for the rest of the body.

Over many years of observing various strength and flexibility programs, I have found that Larry Starr, trainer of the Cincinnati Reds baseball team, has developed a clear, concise philosophy toward training. Starr points out that strength "1) increases the prevention of injury; 2) increases muscular endurance, thus enabling the player to compete for greater duration without fatigue; and 3) increases the playing lifetime of a player." (After all, look at Grandpa Gordie Howe, a superbly conditioned athlete playing with his sons for the NHL New England Whalers, after reaching the ripe old age of fifty!)

The Reds' trainer also states that the best equipment today, for strength training as well as joint flexibility, is the Nautilus time machine. I agree wholeheartedly, as I had the chance recently to visit West Point Military Academy and watch their hockey team work with the machines. I will not go into detail as to the machine's functions, as it should be used under professional supervision, but merely describe in general its advantages and shortcomings, according to Larry Starr. Here are some NHL pros working out on gym machines (Figs. 50–53).

The Nautilus is not the only equipment available. Barbells and dumbbells have an advantage, in that they can be used in the average home (while the average family can hardly afford or house a Nautilus!). They are slightly less efficient than the Nautilus in building strength, but are perfectly adequate. (They are also limited in developing "full-range joint flexibility" according to Starr.)

Another piece of equipment is the Universal Gym. It is, according to Starr's research, less efficient than either the Nautilus or barbells, but is still adequate for the average athlete in strength training.

Finally, if the athlete simply cannot go to the expense of either buying dumbbells and barbells, or going to a gym which has either the Nautilus or Universal Gym, there are actually several household items which can be used for strength exercises.

For young athletes and beginners who are uncertain how intense they wish their strength training to be, I recommend the book *Getting Strong* by Kathryn Lance (Bobbs Merrill, 1978). Don't be put off by the fact that the book is geared to women (after all, women's involvement in sports is growing at an astronomical rate, even in hockey), because its importance lies in the fact that Ms. Lance gives a complete list of household items and their weights (i.e., large tin cans) for strength building, as well as a well-thought-out program of gradual exercise which is perfect for the novice, regardless of age or sex. Let's be realistic, most of us have never lifted anything heavier than a fork on a regular basis.

If the athlete opts for regular weight lifting and strength training, then I recommend that it be undertaken with the guidance of a well-trained coach at a good gymnasium, where individual needs and capabilities will be taken into consideration.

Here are general guidelines for strength training as established by Larry Starr:

> When establishing a strength-training program it must be remembered that strength is general, not specific. You should work all joints throughout their complete line of action. It must also be remembered that many injuries are caused by an improper balance between agonist (muscles which move a body part) and antagonist (muscles which oppose that movement). For example, when strengthening the thigh muscles, if we devoted all our time to the quadriceps and ignored the hamstrings, the ultimate result would be numerous injuries to the hamstrings. This would be true for hips, back, shoulders, elbows, and ankles. . . .

and

When doing the program, start out with a relatively light weight, so that you are sure to execute the exercise in the proper manner. Lifting a weight is not enough, regardless of the amount of weight. How you lift a weight is a factor of far greater importance. You should be able to do at least 8 good repetitions. If you cannot do 8, then the weight is too heavy. If you can do 12 or more, then the weight is too light and you should add another five to ten pounds. The program should stress complete range of motion, attempting to obtain a stretch before executing the movement.

With these pointers in mind, Starr then suggests the following fundamentals when doing each exercise:

1. Do all repetitions through the complete range of motion.
2. Do all repetitions by raising on a 1-2 count, lowering on a 1-2-3-4 count.
3. Do all repetitions slowly, making sure to pause briefly at the fully contracted position and at the starting position.
4. Do all repetitions concentrating on form; weight increases will follow accordingly.
5. Do all repetitions in a smooth and controlled manner, completely avoiding all heaving and jerking of the weights.
6. Do all repetitions competing against yourself, not other players.

It is also necessary to do a broad range of flexibility exercises in addition to strength training. I am sure that everyone has at some time heard the term "musclebound." This term can become only too real if the athlete is obsessed with building up ever larger musculature. Hugely developed muscles exercised only through weight lifting can become almost completely inflexible. Here are some flexibility exercises I recommend to my students. Each exercise should be repeated ten times unless otherwise indicated.

Hamstring Stretch

Stand up straight. Cross one leg in front of the other, but keep the feet together. Bend over on a slow two-count, keeping the legs straight, touch the toes, hold for a count of four and back up. Do this with each leg.

Achilles Tendon Stretch

Step forward with one foot (about 15 inches). Keeping the heel flat on the floor, bend over, touch the toes and hold for a count of four. Repeat with the other leg forward.

Toe Touches

Stand with the feet 18 to 24 inches apart, hands on hips. Bend down, keeping your knees straight, touch your left toe with your right hand three times, then both hands between your feet three times, then your left hand to your right toe three times. When one hand touches the opposite foot, keep the other hand on your hip. Do this entire sequence five times.

Hip and Groin Stretch

Step forward with one foot and bend that knee as far as possible. Stretch the other leg behind you as far as you can, keeping the foot flat on the floor. Hold for a count of four. Switch legs with each ten repetitions.

Groin Stretch, Buddy System (two people working together)

Two persons sit facing on the floor, putting their legs in the spread-eagle position, with the soles of each other's feet touching. Take hold of each other's wrists and rock back and forth toward each other, ten times in each direction. This rocking will pull the legs even further apart, stretching the thighs, groins and even the back muscles.

Back and Groin Stretch

Sit on the floor and bring your feet toward your crotch, touching your soles together. Holding your ankles to keep the feet together, bend over and try to touch your head to your feet. Bend over twenty repetitions, trying to get the head closer to the feet each time, but without bouncing or jerking.

Squats

Stand with the feet 18 to 24 inches apart, hands on hips. Now squat until your buttocks almost rest on your heels, which will rise as you sink. Then rise again slowly, making the entire squat and rise a continuous motion.

Knee Pulls

Lie flat on your back and raise one knee, touching it to your chest if possible. Take the knee in your hands and attempt to touch your head to the knee. Twenty repetitions each knee.

Trunk Twists

Stand with feet slightly apart, arms straight out in front of you at shoulder height. Twist the entire upper torso, with the arms stretched out to your sides, first to the left, then to the right, trying to turn the arms further to the side each time. Twenty repetitions.

Arm Circles

Stand straight with feet a few inches apart and hold the arms straight out to the side at shoulder height. Now move the arms in very small circles for ten rotations, then in large circles for ten rotations.

Kicks

Stand with the feet together and the arms straight out in front at shoulder height. Kick one leg up, trying to reach the arms, then repeat with the other leg. Then, from the same position, kick one leg, held straight, first to the front, then to the sides, then to the back, as high in each direction as possible. Do the entire sequence five times with each leg, don't let the kicking leg touch the floor between kicks, and don't lower your arms to meet the kick—try to get the leg up to the arms!

An important area where flexibility is needed in hockey—especially for goalies—but which is generally neglected, is the eyes. Players have begun to realize, however, that the quicker the reflexes of the eyes, the better the chance for keeping track of the puck or the opponent.

Dr. Leon Revien, for thirty years a Long Island, New York, optometrist, and Director of the Athletes' Visual Skills Training Center in Great Neck, New York, has developed machines and equipment for testing and increasing the visual skills and reflexes of athletes. I have used these machines myself, as have several of the New York Islanders, and I can vouch for their worth.

Obviously, few of you are going to be within range of Dr. Revien and his equipment, nor are there many places like the Athletes' Visual Skills Training Center in the rest of North America. So I asked Dr. Revien for some home exercises to be performed by anyone which will increase eye flexibility and strength.

Dr. Revien recommends a very simple exercise to increase overall eye muscle strength. Simply sit in a relaxed position and, keeping the head stationary, rotate the eyeballs in the largest possible circle, first clockwise for several rotations, then counterclockwise. Do this rotation strongly enough that you actually feel the pull on the eye muscles as you rotate the eyeballs.

Next, "Play Marbles." This entails taking a small carton or box, such as a shoe box or small grocery carton, and placing several different colored marbles in it. Holding the box, rotate it causing the marbles to move. Then, without moving your head, attempt to follow one or two marbles with your eyes as they move through the others.

Try an exercise Dr. Revien calls "Shooting License." While riding in a car, try to spot one particular digit, for instance "3", on every license plate you see. Next, look for a pre-selected two-digit combination, such as "42." Finally, move up to reading whole license plate numbers with one look.

The "Eye-Screen Cone" takes a little more work, but is good for improving what is called "depth of field" vision. Tie two strings to two trees or poles that are anywhere from 20 to 50 feet apart. Stand between the trees with the strings in your hands and then back off until the strings are taut. You will be standing at the apex of a cone, or triangle. Now, put the strings up to your eyes and attempt to sight *simultaneously* along both *strings* without moving your head. This may sound impossible—asking each eye to move in an opposing direction—but in fact, it will increase your peripheral vision and the amount of detail you can remember in the whole area between the two trees or poles. If you stand closer to the trees, your eyes will have to encompass a wider viewing area, while if you stand further back, the areas will be narrower but deeper.

Dr. Revien points out that under normal conditions almost 80 percent of the information a body uses comes through vision, while the body's movements are almost continuously made through spatial judgments. He claims that spatial judgment, a function of vision, is a learned skill and can be both acquired and improved throughout life.

Dr. Revien also avers that he has found no limits to the development potential of an individual's visual skills. In other words, no matter how good the eyes, there is always room for improvement.

New York Islanders' ace goalie, Glenn Resch, used Dr. Revien's machines and said, "Prior to the training, the puck came in and it looked like a 'BB.' Now it comes in and it looks like a grapefruit!"

If you wish to go further into Revien's eye training, I recommend you read *Sports Vision*, by Dr. Leon Revien and Mark Gabor (Harper & Row, 1979).

Some of you may be slightly puzzled after reading this chapter—wondering why I didn't sit down and give you "Barbara Williams's Gospel on How to Eat, Train, Win, And/Or Live Longer." Why, you may wonder, did I tell you to go one place for diet, another for strength training, and yet another to get your eyes in shape?

I did it for good reason. As I said before, I am not a nutritionist, nor am I a coach at a health spa. The only "gospel" I preach is power skating, and if you are interested in becoming as good a hockey skater and player as you possibly can, then the only "gospel" you should follow is that which develops the specific skills which are unique to that sport.

For the rest—diet, conditioning and exercise—there is no one system which does everything, nor one single method which is perfect. Health, diet, exercise, and conditioning are things which you must practice and consider for yourself with your own individual needs and desires in mind. Pushing yourself to extremes, or going "whole hog" for some new system is not the way to take good care of yourself: don't make a "cult" out of your physical development techniques—just form good habits from them. Common sense, careful consideration, and moderation will stand you in good stead through a lifetime.

RIGHTING SOME WRONGS FOR A GOOD BODY POSITION 4

The average professional hockey player skates two to three miles each game, while a "superstar" might log as much as four miles on the ice during three periods of play! No matter how well-exercised that player is off the ice, or during off-season, if he does not have a good skating position, those miles will all feel as though they were skated uphill!

Unfortunately, many young hockey players spend most of their ice time trying to perfect the slapshot, rather than remembering that hockey centers first and forever around skating. Skating skills can be improved, and if the young skaters would simply stop for a moment and think, they would realize that it's never too late to correct their skating technique.

Virtually every hockey player I have ever trained or observed in action has had some fault of body position or skating technique, some of which can be corrected relatively easily. Other problems may take long, corrective practice, but usually improvement will be worth the battle. In this chapter I will describe what I call "universal" faults in body position and then offer—in layman's terms—a corrective procedure for each fault.

The first rule I want to stress is that *anything* done in skating should be done slowly at first, with speed being built up only gradually. This is also the case regarding the number of times an exercise should be performed; start with a few, then gradually increase the number.

Most of you, I'm sure, have at some time seen a hockey player "rev up" in a heated game: his legs milling, arms pumping, teeth gritted, face twisted, head down, he lunges down ice. The thought is that by "bunching up" to push off, the skater is concentrating as much energy as possible into getting a fast start; oddly enough, nothing could be further from the truth —that action is nearly all wasted energy!

Tensing the muscles into tight knots doesn't allow them to function to their fullest. The trick is to relax, yet be able to increase speed at will.

HEADS UP!

The primary "sin" being committed by the churning player we have just described is that his head is down, his eyes looking at his churning skates as he pushes off. Unfortunately, this habit of holding the head down while skating is often reinforced when the skater learns to check and puck-handle. Many youngsters who have already developed the tendency begin to watch the puck constantly while stick-handling, with the head once again always down. When they learn checking, they compound the problem by assuming that charging in on an opponent with the head held down will increase their thrust.

Skating, checking, and puck-handling with the head

Figure 54

Figure 55

held consistently down can be absolutely disastrous, leading to severe neck and back injuries—at the least. Parents, if you see this happening in a hockey clinic, point it out to the coach, so he/she can correct the tendency immediately.

As you can see in Figure 54, the child is skating with his head down, in a vain attempt to speed up. Strangely, what feels natural in skating is often the wrong move to make, as in this instance; it "feels" as though you can gain speed by putting the head down, but it simply is not so.

Notice that the player in Figure 55 has his head up, and more importantly, his head is held up in a relaxed manner, for holding up your head in a rigid and fixed fashion can be just as futile and dangerous as holding it down!

The primary reason for holding your head up is obvious: to see where you are skating, to see where the puck is at all times, to follow the action, to avert danger, to pass, and to shoot. The head-up position with resulting good eye flexibility is so important, in fact, that some professional hockey players have begun to take eye training, as previously mentioned in "Getting Into Shape."

Figure 56   There are two basic exercises for curing the "head down syndrome": one is a bit slow but easy; the other is fast but a little like shock treatment.

The parent or coach should stand to the side of the player, and blow the whistle as the signal for the skater to push off. Then the coach should give silent signals for his next moves. If the skater doesn't have his eyes on you, he is not going to see what is expected of him, and after a couple of mixed-up or missed signals, he'll get the message and start to keep his head up.

If the skater's problem is more chronic, then the shock treatment will be required, but do it carefully. Stand aside slightly and give the same whistle signal for the skater to push off, but immediately after doing so, skate directly in front of the offender. I guarantee that he will take a swift, hard bounce right off you, usually landing on his well-padded posterior! One bounce is usually enough to get the point across, and with proper equipment on, the poor skater has suffered nothing more severe than one good fall in exchange for one quick lesson well learned.

THE UPPER TORSO . . . OR "PISA" . . . DON'T LEAN!

Take a look at Figure 56. It looks like the personification of a gazelle in flight, correct? Wrong! What we have here is one very badly balanced skater who has merely to be tapped to end up in a battered heap, as is about to happen in Figure 57.

Skating while leaning too far forward with the torso extended in front of the skates is another common bad habit many skaters fall into, again because leaning forward "feels" as though you are going faster. It may help a racer extend his/her chest across the finish wire,

Figure 57: *"Hey, Robby, I said 'Lean forward,' but that's ridiculous," says Barbara to actor Robby Benson, then training for his starring role in the movie, "Ice Castles." (Photo by Columbia Pictures/Paul Schumach.)*

but a hockey skater is not attempting to win a foot race, he/she is trying to maintain speed and balance on a very slippery surface. The only way ultimately to accomplish this is to skate with the torso held erect over the skates, in a balanced position, as Figure 58 indicates. Not only does this posture increase speed, balance, and agility, but an upright torso leaves room for the heart and lungs to perform best. Leaning forward simply cramps both of these organs, thereby greatly hindering endurance. The proper position of the torso, then, is *slightly* forward, so that the shoulder lines up over the knee and toe of the skate.

To correct this fault of too much forward lean, line the class up in a "good hockey position," then blow the whistle as a signal to start skating. If anyone is holding the torso too far forward, skate up from the side and give him/her a *slight* shove. The youngster will immediately lose balance and break stride, hopefully learning the lesson without falling.

I emphasize "slight" shove here, because of one experience I had when I first taught sixteen-year-olds. One young man simply refused to straighten up his torso, continuing to do his off-balance imitation of winged Mercury. Finally, I skated to his side, and in an excess of frustrated fervor, gave the lad a hearty shove, whereupon he promptly toppled over. He was uninjured physically, but his pride had suffered a great fall, both before his peers, and worse yet, as it happened, before his highly protective mother. The boy's mother immediately began berating me from the sidelines, accusing me of everything from brutality to child abuse. Mind you, the boy was unhurt and stood almost one foot taller and one hundred pounds heavier than this "brutal" coach! However, I wasted the better part of some very expensive ice time placating her.

A minute or two later, I received a violent shove from my left side. Had I not been skating in a "good hockey position," I'd have been on my tail with a few loose teeth. Needless to say, it was our disgruntled

Figure 58: *here we have a well-balanced skater.*

sixteen-year-old retaliating, but the attempted revenge served a very good purpose. The poor kid was utterly stunned when I didn't fall over in a broken heap, but merely rocked on my skates for a second! We all learned a lesson, and while he skated a lot straighter after the episode, I decided that a "slight" shove was the better part of future wisdom.

Figure 59: *this boy is standing too straight, making him a "push-over" prone to knee injuries.*

BEND THOSE KNEES . . . PLEASE!

One of the most crucial faults in skating is not bending the knees sufficiently (Figure 59). The taller the player, the more awkward it will feel, at first, to skate with a well-bent knee. However, it is impossible to exert enough pressure on the blade edge while skating unless the knees are bent properly.

Well-bent knees play a key role in taking turns, pivoting, crossing-over, stopping, and taking off, not to mention taking a check. Standing up straight literally makes the skater a pushover, and knee injuries are one of the most prevalent in hockey today.

Many of my skating students tease me about keeping the knees bent, pointing out that it's simple for me, being only five feet, two inches tall and born "close to the ground." But my exhortations to them to keep those knees bent are mild compared to what Eddie Shore used to propose! Shore was known for his myriad, seemingly crazy but innovative techniques, such as having his players learn tap dancing to increase their agility, and he also was an early proponent of the well-bent knee.

Shore often coaxed his players into bending their knees by describing the position as ". . . sitting in the outhouse, but trying not to touch the seat!" You'll have to admit, it gives a pretty graphic picture of what he wanted to accomplish! It is possible, though, to teach this position without bringing the outhouse in. . . .

Line the players up in good hockey position, head up, torso over the skates and knee well bent. Then, blow the whistle, and watch for straight legs as they perform. Skate to the side and just slightly behind the offender, and tap the back of the knee "crotch" with the stick. Don't whack the skater, just tap. It may take some repetition, but ultimately it will work.

THE FEET: A FIRM FOUNDATION

Another common problem with many a skater is the habit of moving with the feet too far apart. Wide placement "feels" more secure to many, but skating with the feet more than shoulder width apart cuts down on the thrust of the skate and lessens forward motion. In other words, feet too wide apart waste energy by forcing the skater to move almost sideways instead of forward (Fig. 60, left).

If the skater skates with his/her feet too far apart he/she is also in danger of performing an involuntary "splitz" on the ice when checked, shoved, or even when stopping. Conversely, if the feet are less than shoulder width apart, the skater will be in constant imbalance, especially sideways, and can easily be toppled over. (Fig. 60, middle). Keeping the feet shoulder width apart is the optimum position for stability, balance, and extension or thrust (Fig. 60, right).

Shore was known to tie the ankles of his skaters together when their feet were too far apart, and I also

Figure 60: *note that the player on the left has the skates much too widely spaced, while the middle skater is unbalanced by a narrow stance. The feet should be a shoulder width apart for greatest stability and balance, as the player on the right illustrates.*

Figure 61: *the "high-kicker" wastes speed, thrust, and balance.*

Figure 62: *the thrusting skate should be only 2–3 inches off the ice as it follows through.*

knew one coach who used to hook one skate of the hapless player who held his feet too widely spaced, causing him to sink helplessly into a splitz. Both techniques can cause injury, however, and there is no need for such dire methods.

In many hockey clinics videotape replay is a major aid for pointing out faults to skaters. If your hockey school has no visual aids, then pointing out the fault with constant correction and repetition is the main curative technique. If the coach pushes lightly on the shoulder of a skater who holds his/her feet too close together, the fault will be immediately apparent. A variation of the same "cure" can be used on the skater with too widely spaced feet, by applying a slight downward push on his/her shoulder, but without causing him to perform the splitz.

THE FEET AGAIN:
NO HIGH KICKERS NEED APPLY

As you can see in Figure 61, the player is kicking his feet up too high with each stroke of the skate, another common poor trait. This is caused largely because after the hard thrust of the skate, it "feels" as though the proper reaction is to raise the foot equally as hard. Wrong. The "high kicker" wastes energy as well as losing speed and thrust, not to mention putting himself off balance.

The higher the foot from the ice, the longer it takes to return it to skating position, thus losing speed and thrust. And it is only logical that if one foot is high up in the air when a player receives a push or shove, he can easily be toppled before he gets that foot back on the ice to stabilize his balance again. Figure 62 shows the proper distance (2–3 inches) the foot should be raised from the ice surface in a normal thrust.

Some coaches actually attach small weights on the players' skates, in an attempt to keep the feet close to the ice, but I have found that this approach doesn't really work all that well. In fact, after the weights are removed, the players often raise their feet too high from a habitual reaction to having worn the weights! I find that reminding the skater that he is raising his feet too high after each thrust will usually be sufficient, although it sometimes takes time and many reminders.

PUSHING OFF WITH THE TOE: OR, NO BALLERINAS ALLOWED!

Some hockey players are known as "runners" or "toe dancers" because they only use the toe of the skate when pushing off or thrusting (Fig. 63). This fault is easiest to spot in the push-off, when the player gets up on the toes, churns the legs and "gallops" down the ice rather than skating. It looks as though tremendous effort is being utilized to get a fast, strong start, but in fact there is a huge loss of thrust with this method.

Videotape is again a good diagnostic tool, if available, particularly when comparison between various skaters' styles can be made. If replay is unavailable, there is a simple exercise to correct the tendency.

Line up the skaters in good hockey position, blow the whistle, and have the skaters simply push each skate to the side, the weight on the ball of the foot, until there is an accumulation of snow to each side. "Piling up snow" is always a sure sign of proper weight being applied to the thrust, and if that telltale sign is not there after the skater pushes, then the weight is not on the ball of the foot. I use this drill on my little tykes, and when the older kids find out they're doing a "tykes" exercise, they correct the fault, fast!

THE STICK: YOU AIN'T GOT A THING IF YOU AIN'T GOT THE RIGHT SWING

Before moving to problems in skating with the stick, let's look at common faults in choice of stick size. It is

Figure 63: *this fellow has pushed off with the toe rather than with the whole blade, with a huge loss of thrust.*

Figure 64: *the proper length stick touches the chin or lips when the skater, wearing skates, holds it perpendicular to the ice.*

very popular with some youngsters to carry a stick which is actually too short for them. As mentioned earlier, the stick should reach at least to the chin or lips when the skater (wearing skates) holds it out, resting on the ice, in front of him perpendicular to the ice (Fig. 64).

If the stick is any shorter than this, it will cause the skater to lean over too far, resulting in imbalance and totally disrupting the good hockey position. A stick which is too long will have the reverse effect, causing the player to be too upright, with the legs too straight. The extra length is also very awkward to handle.

As far as skating with the stick, the single worst problem while moving is swinging the stick too high (Fig. 65), which is extremely dangerous. That high-flying stick is not only akin to a poleax for anyone else on the ice, but it will waste the skater's energy and cause imbalance.

Figure 65: *the player who swings the stick too high while skating becomes a dangerous person.*

I will never forget the night I was teaching a small class of boys in power skating. I was explaining to them that they shouldn't skate down the ice "looking like an ape swinging its arms" when all of a sudden I felt someone tap me on the shoulder (Fig. 66). As I turned and looked up I almost had a heart attack: there stood a huge ape, almost seven feet tall, with a hockey stick in his hand! I stood in utter shock for a moment and then we all burst out laughing (Fig. 67). Under the ape costume was a good friend, Larry Cangro, whom I taught in the senior men's league. Larry wanted to get even with me for always thundering at him to stop skating down ice like an ape. From that night on, whenever I am about to make that comparison of some youngster skating and waving his stick in the air, I look carefully over my shoulder first, just to make sure that King Kong isn't skating behind me.

Certain talented professional hockey players have inadvertently contributed to another common fault with less experienced skaters. Many of the pros skate on the ice or carry the puck while holding the stick with only one hand. With a truly good skater this can be at times useful, as in fending off or blocking an opponent with one hand while carrying the puck with the other. It

Figure 66: *there I was telling the kids not to "skate down the ice like apes" when suddenly I felt a tap on my shoulder. . . . (Photo by Kevin Rich.)*

Figure 67: *when I realized it was a former student of mine, and not King Kong, we all had a good laugh. (Photo by Kevin Rich.)*

also indicates, in an expert skater, that the stick is not a "crutch," that he is not placing his weight on the stick.

But in the novice hockey player skating with only one hand on the stick is ridiculous. The one-handed stick hold results in lack of control when handling the puck, and worse, makes it almost impossible to control a hard pass. Taking a hard pass with only one hand will mean, nine times out of ten, that the puck bounces right off and into the hands of the opposition.

Rhythm is the key to skating with the stick. The slight movement of the stick when skating in normal stride should be *with* the weight distribution of the body as shown back in Figure 62, page 64. Notice that the weight of the skater is directly on the right side of the body, with the shoulders and knees in line with the toe of the skating foot. The stick is on that side also. In Figure 61 (p. 64), the stick is moving in a counter-productive fashion, against the player's weight (i.e., weight over extended right foot, but stick to left).

SUMMARY: IT'S ALL IN YOUR HEAD!

We have been discussing problems connected with the movement and positioning of the body, but one of the primary problems on the ice is found *in* the head, not in how the skater is *holding* his head! One of hockey's (or any sport's) most devastating bad habits concerns the poor mental attitude of a player, toward himself and toward his game.

Some of the many skaters I trained with in youth hockey had already been labeled as "trouble-makers" before we started to work together. They were constantly starting fights, and were often thrown out of games. I have found that in most cases these hardened "troublemakers" were lashing out from frustration, pure frustration often caused by a personal failing. If that young skater can't get to the puck because he's too slow, or can't control the puck when he does get to it, because of poor balance and technique, then it's no surprise that he will be tempted to crack the stick over other skaters' heads! Thinking positively, while learning proper power skating techniques, can make a world of difference to the troubled player. If the skater firmly believes that he can never improve his skating or his game, then he will always do poorly. So it is necessary to do some curing of mental faults, too—some positive thinking drills!

If there is an outstanding player on the opposition, and you think to yourself, "There's no way this guy is going to get by me," believe me, it's going to be a lot harder for that fellow to get around you than if you say, "Ah, forget it, I could never catch this guy." You certainly won't if you believe you can't. I recommend a certain book, especially to the older hockey players, which I think can be a tremendous help in building a positive attitude and creating confidence. It's called *Psycho-Cybernetics*, by Dr. Maxwell Maltz (Pocket Books, 1979). One of the toughest defensemen I ever witnessed was Larry Zeidel who played with the Philadelphia Flyers when they were first created in the NHL expansion of the 1967–68 season. Larry was already a long time veteran of the minor leagues when expansion came about, but it looked as though all the new teams were going to pass Larry by when they drafted players. Larry had read *Psycho-Cybernetics*, however, and he believed in himself—he *knew* he was good enough for the big leagues. So Larry made up a resume of his talents and his experience, and sent it to all of the new teams. The Flyers brass were so impressed at the confidence and stick-to-itiveness of Zeidel that they took him on, and Larry made the team. Not only that, he became a real asset to a raw bunch of youngsters.

It always pays to think positively. So, if you come across a drill or two that you can't do right away, just say to yourself, "I'm going to master these moves, no matter what."

The sky's the limit!

5 WARM-UPS

In the two previous chapters we discussed getting into shape year-round and correcting some common faults in skating. Some of you may think that "warm-ups" are the same thing as the "getting into shape" exercises, or the drills used to correct faults. But there is an important distinction to be made here. Getting (and keeping) your body in shape is a year-round job and is of course crucial for building strength, stamina, wind, and also for avoiding injury. The drills we discussed for correcting skating faults are directed specifically at specific problems or bad habits. Warm-ups are the exercises every skater *must* do either on or off the ice before skating; they are an essential part of good skating, preparing your muscles for the heavy, sudden demands placed on them by the sport.

Don't ever get into the habit of skating directly onto the ice and into a game or training session without performing some warm-ups. No matter how well conditioned your body is, you must prepare it, "warm it up," for the demands which hockey playing or skating will put on it. There is such a premium on ice time in most rinks in this country, you will often find that you cannot do warm-ups on ice before your actual skating or playing session, but nevertheless, you should spend at least twenty minutes slowly loosening up your muscles.

The following warm-up exercises can be performed both on and off the ice, although naturally it would be preferable to do them in skates on the ice. It is a fine idea for the really young hockey player to begin doing these warm-ups too, since it teaches them discipline and starts them off with good habits, but warm-ups are especially important for the teenage skater and older.

Warm-ups are a key element in preventing injury during play, but they must be done properly, or you can injure yourself while doing them! As with any exercise or drill, they should be done slowly at first, and the number of times you perform each exercise should be increased gradually also, depending on the judgment of your coach and yourself, as to how far your body needs to be loosened up and readied for action. I generally recommend starting out by doing each exercise two to three times, working up to five to six times.

GROIN STRETCH I

Glide forward on one skate (the left skate in our Figure 68) with the stick placed on the ice in front, in the same hand as the gliding foot. Bend the gliding knee as much as possible, until your buttocks are only inches from the ice. At the same time extend the right leg back, keeping the *whole skate blade* flat on the ice as you do so. Your back will be slightly arched, but basically the torso remains erect and the head is definitely held up, eyes looking forward. Remember, glide on the flat of the left blade, as you "drag" the whole of the other blade—do not put your weight on the toe of the

Figure 68: *the important moves to remember in the "groin stretch" are: keep the weight on the ball of the gliding foot, and "drag" the whole blade of the backward-extended skate.*

gliding skate, and do not let the heel of your dragging skate rise from the ice.

Correct execution is most important, since the groin muscles are easily subject to pulls and tears. I am sure most of you have heard or seen many a hockey player forced to leave a game because of a "groin pull." The poor player usually misses several games thereafter, too. So learn this exercise well and perform it very carefully!

GROIN STRETCH II: STICKS OVER THE HEAD

In this groin exercise, the skater moves slowly down the ice, feet shoulder width apart, stick raised over the head (Fig. 69). At the command "legs apart," the player separates the legs, pressing on the inside edges, as far as is comfortably possible. While the legs are separated, and *straight*, the skater bends over, touching the stick to the toes of the skates (Fig. 70).

Finally the skater brings the feet straight back to their original shoulder width apart position, as rapidly as possible. Do not glide the feet back, but snap them

Figure 69: *(Photo by Kevin Rich.)*

Figure 70: *(Photo by Kevin Rich.)*

Figure 71

Figure 72

back as quickly as is comfortably possible, and raise the stick once more over the head, ready to repeat the exercise.

I stress "snapping" the feet back because this stretch is most effective not only when you separate the feet, but because of the rapid return of the feet. You gain only half the worth of the exercise if you glide the feet back.

HAMSTRING STRETCH: STICKS OVER THE HEAD

Glide down the ice, feet closer together than normal, stick held over your head (Fig. 71). At the signal, bend over and touch the toes with the stick (Fig. 72). Try to keep your legs as straight as possible when you bend, as this is what actually stretches the long hamstring muscles in the upper part of your legs. Also keep your weight on the back half of your blades and do not allow yourself to lean forward onto the toes of your skates, or you will end up on one very badly bruised face! This exercise can be performed when gliding either backward or forward.

TOE TOUCHES: STICKS IN BACK

Place the stick across the back of your shoulders, a hand at each end, and stand with your feet shoulder width apart. Next, lean your body slightly forward, bending your knees only as far as necessary to touch first your right hand to your left skate and then the left hand to the right skate (Figs. 73 and 74). This toe touch is not easy to perform, and I find that most hockey players will do it on the flats of their blades. Instead, you should press on the inside edges of the skates, and attempt to feel a real thrust each time you touch a toe. Be sure to keep your weight on the back of the blades while you press on the inside edges, however,

Figure 73: *(Photo by Kevin Rich.)*

Figure 74: *(Photo by Kevin Rich.)*

or you will pitch forward into disaster when you try to touch your toes. The primary purpose of this toe touch exercise is to stretch and loosen the waist, arms, shoulders and back muscles.

TWISTS: STICKS IN BACK

As in the previous exercise, place the stick across your shoulders, a hand at each end of the stick, feet shoulder width apart. At the signal, twist your shoulders while staying in a basically erect posture. Twist each way as far as you are able and give an extra push at the end of each twist (Fig. 75), but don't jerk. This exercise loosens everything from the waist up. Each time you twist, your skates will press on their inside edges.

Figure 75: *(Photo by Kevin Rich.)*

Figure 76 *"Remember, don't cheat on the leg lifts, Tommy—bring your leg up to the stick, don't lower the stick to your skate!"*

LEG LIFTS: STICKS IN FRONT

Hold the stick in front of you at shoulder height. Now raise your right foot, while balancing on your left, to touch the stick (Fig. 76). Then repeat the exercise lifting the left foot to the stick while balancing on the right.

This is one of those exercises that lends itself to a sort of "cheating." What happens often is that a hockey skater will lower the stick to the partially raised foot, instead of properly bringing the foot all the way up to shoulder height. Granted, it is difficult to lift that leg up so high, but otherwise the exercise is useless.

Figure skaters have no trouble performing this leg lift, and I have a feeling that it is because they are encouraged and expected to perform graceful balletlike movements. Hockey players, however, are expected to be masculine, not graceful, and anything which smacks of ballet is something they have never in their lives been encouraged to do. Thus, I find the best way to present this exercise is matter-of-factly, without any discussion about ballet or "feminine" moves. The skaters can achieve the shoulder height lift more easily and quickly. Just remind any "cheater" who is lowering his stick to his toe instead of the reverse, that in football place-kicking and punting require the same sort of ability to kick over the head. In karate, as well, the kick, a high one, is as important as any move in the whole art. Once the correct height is achieved, there will be a healthy loosening of the groin, hamstring, and quadricep (front thigh) muscles.

In all of the previous warm-up exercises I have found that many, many hockey players, right up to the professional level, have learned them incorrectly—that, in fact, many coaches do not know how to teach these exercises properly. Bad habits can lead ultimately to torn muscles, so please watch, read, and perform cautiously and exactly. The watchwords are: do the warm-ups slowly, gradually, building up the repetitions to the desired level.

Robert Browning once said, "Let your reach exceed your grasp," which is excellent advice for your brain and your ambitions, but not so good for your muscles! Never push them beyond what you—and your coach—feel is a comfortable limit, or painful, pulled muscles will be the price you pay. Remember, you are striving for stamina and conditioning, not strain.

GOALIE WARM-UPS

Goalies have their own special system of warm-ups, which are done *before* they join the regular warm-up. Here are the most important goalie warm-ups.

Touching Head to Ice
(Fig. 77). This warm-up is difficult to execute, and you should bend back slowly and carefully, gradually work-

Figure 77

ing your way down to touching the head on the ice. The key is to bend back only as far as you safely feel you can pull your body (keeping the spine straight) back up again without strain. If performed correctly, this warm-up will loosen the thigh, groin, abdominal, back, and neck muscles.

Splitz

(Fig. 78). This warm-up loosens the calf, thigh, and groin muscles, as well as the knee ligaments. The important thing to remember is to move down into the splitz position slowly; it will be almost impossible for you to move as low as our illustration indicates, at first, and if you bounce or jerk down into the splitz, you stand a good chance of tearing muscles. You can get out of the splitz by sitting sideways and taking the pressure off your skates, or you can slowly push your skates back together and rise to the standing position, which will loosen the muscles even further, but requires great strength.

One-Pad Stretch

(Fig. 79). This may appear to be one half of a splitz, but this is not the case. First, the left leg in this in-

Figure 78

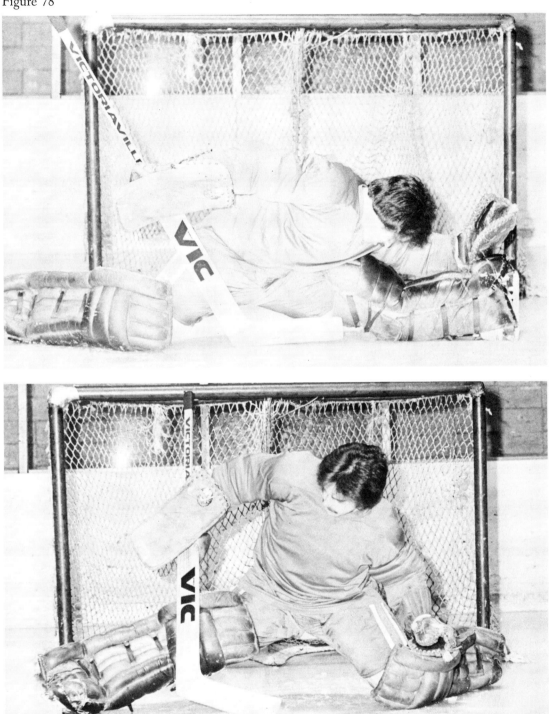

Figure 79

Figure 80

Figure 81

Figure 82

stance is resting on the knee (instead of extending the whole leg back as in the splitz) as the right pad (leg) is extended while keeping the blade flat on the ice (instead of resting on the heel of the skate as in the splitz). This loosens the groin muscles even more than the splitz.

Side Leg Lifts

To further loosen the groin and thigh muscles, the goalie lies on his side with his pads neatly "stacked" on top of one another (Fig. 80). Then he raises the top leg as high as he is able (Fig. 81), keeping it straight. Finally, the leg is slowly lowered (Fig. 82) and without touching the pad on the ice the leg lift is repeated immediately.

Figure 83

Figure 84

Figure 85

Front Leg Lifts

Lie flat on the ice (Fig. 83), then raise the legs approximately two feet off the ice (Fig. 84), separate the pads (Fig. 85), bring them back together and lower the legs. This exercise is excellent for warming up the muscles of the abdomen and buttocks, especially.

Legs in "V" Position

This exercise is really a sitting "toe touch" drill (Fig. 86) and is excellent for the thigh and groin muscles. The goalie sits on the ice, then spreads the legs into a modified "v," bending the head to one knee, and touching the fingers to the foot. Both legs should remain fully extended as the goalie bends first over one leg, then over the other.

Figure 86

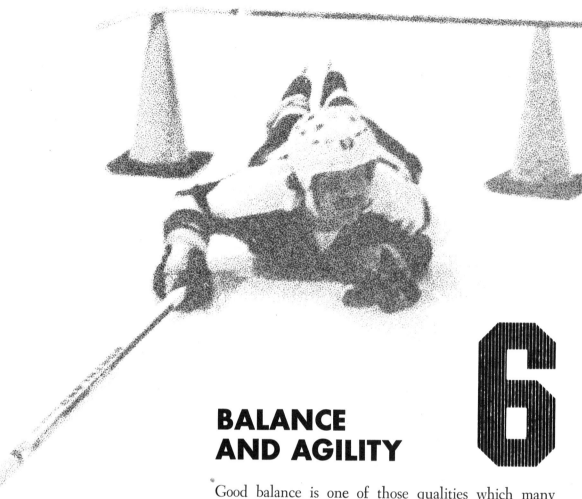

BALANCE AND AGILITY

6

Good balance is one of those qualities which many people think they have from birth, and can never "learn." This might be true in the extreme case of a physical handicap, but normally, balance is a skill which can be developed and which differs greatly from sport to sport.

In skating, the primary challenge is built around the fact that you are performing on an extremely slippery surface on two thin strips of metal. Everything you do relies on your ability to balance your weight so as to remain upright on those two thin strips! You can practice your stick-handling all you want, or do power skating drills until you're blue in the face, but if you can't balance on your blades, there is no chance the NHL will draft you from your hands and knees!

The following balance drills may look very simple, but after you try doing them a couple of times, you'll find out how deceptively difficult they are. In our first illustration, observe Islander forward Bobby Nystrom, who has worked with me for over five years. Bobby is attempting a balance exercise on one foot from a squat, one foot held out in front. Bobby happens to have excellent balance, but as you can see from the following sequence, he has just leaned a bit too far back from the squat position, and is taking a fall! (Fig. 87) Luckily,

Figure 87: *Islander Bobby Nystrom obliges Barbara in a perfect example of poor balance as he deliberately flops while attempting to "shoot the duck." (Photo by Wide World Photos.)*

Figure 88: *Nystrom's teammate, Dave Lewis, executes the same balance drill, "Shooting the Duck," but correctly.*

Bob also has a great sense of humor, and was simply trying to help his coach illustrate a point! Now, observe Islanders' Dave Lewis performing the same drill, known as "Shooting the Duck," with me, correctly this time (Fig. 88).

Another important balance drill is similar to the leg lift we performed as a warm-up exercise. Glide on your skates at moderate speed, with your stick held in both hands at shoulder height in front of you. At the signal, raise your leg in back of you, as straight as possible and as high as is comfortably possible, as shown in Figure 89. At the next signal, swing the leg from behind to the side, keeping the stick always at shoulder height. Finally, at a third signal, swing the leg from sideways to in front of you, but instead of touching your stick as you do in the warm-up exercise, simply hold the leg directly, or straight, in front of you (which will be at hip height). Then repeat with other leg. This is not so easy, as you will find out.

This exercise can be performed while gliding either backward or forward, but the moving skate should not touch the ice at all during the exercise, and the skater must strive to lift one leg as high as the other. This may end up being the most difficult part of the balance exercise because, as we have discussed before, nearly all

Figure 89: *Barbara executes the leg lift balance exercise with her son, Tommy. (Photo by Kevin Rich.)*

Figure 90: *Bobby Bourne and Barbara doing a balancing drill.*

Figure 91: *"Hey, fellas, we were supposed to be working on balance drills, not 'crushing' drills!" exclaims Barbara to Islanders Bobby Bourne and Dave Lewis.*

of us are stronger in one leg than in the other, just as most of us are stronger with one hand than with the other. You can see in the following illustration New York Islander Bobby Bourne doing a one foot balance drill (Figs. 90 and 91).

AGILITY

As we have discussed in the earlier chapters, good skating involves proper balance, speed, coordination, and great expertise. But where would the skater be without agility, the ability to move all that talent down the ice without getting into someone's way? Remember, in hockey everyone is not skating in a nice, regular circle around the rink, keeping a discreet distance from each other. A great deal of what hockey is all about is avoiding somebody else charging at you under very trying circumstances! Even after you have learned the basic skills of skating well, it still takes time and a lot of practice to develop real agility on the ice.

These agility drills do not cover the areas of stick and puck-handling—these arts are for actual hockey playing, but they will add maneuverability to your power skating. Full equipment is absolutely mandatory in these drills—not only for safety's sake, but also for conditioning the body to wearing equipment under game conditions. The exercises consist of a series of falls, rolls, jumps, and other similar body movements, and they can be done on the ice as well as off, for the most part. As with the other drills, they begin on a relatively simple level and increase in difficulty.

"SLIDING INTO HOME PLATE"

As shown in Figure 92, the skater comes down the ice and slides under the two cones. The head should be held up throughout the exercise and after sliding under the stick, the skater should return to an upright position as quickly as possible.

THE "ANYTHING GOES" DRILL

This exercise is actually a lot of fun, although it looks a bit chaotic. Several players should get into a large

Figure 92

Figure 93: *(Photo by Kevin Rich.)*

Figure 94

Figure 95

circle and skate in all different directions, at random—backward and forward, in, out, and sideways, as shown in Figure 93.

The whole purpose of this random skating is to practice avoiding hitting each other. If you manage it the first time, it is a real indication of agility. I'll clue you in to a couple of important things: first, it is almost impossible to skate randomly through a lot of other skating bodies unless your knees are bent properly. I can guarantee you'll never maneuver around those rapidly moving objects with stiff knees. Also, heads *must* be up and *sticks* down at all times—things are *too* close for bad habits.

DROP ROLLS

Figure 94 shows a skater doing a One Knee Drop. While skating at full speed, the skater drops first to one knee and then to the other, alternating. Many coaches have skaters switch from one knee to the other as they cross the lines (blue/red/blue) on a hockey rink, but I have found that using a whistle to signal dropping and switching is preferable. The whistle is better because it helps develop quicker reflexes—if the skater is waiting for that whistle controlled by an outside source, rather than simply watching as the lines go by, they drop and switch considerably faster. The whole purpose of the knee drop is to learn to get up rapidly from a fall under game circumstances. Defensemen can also block shots with knee drops.

Figure 95 demonstrates the Two Knee Drop—the same drill, but with both knees at once.

JUMPS

Jumping may sound scary at first—the thought of both feet leaving the ice at once is always frightening, but all my drills involving jumps are really very simple, and are graduated in such a way as to build confidence, rather than to frighten. Jumping exercises are designed to teach hockey players how to jump rapidly over a stick, a glove, or another hockey player, if necessary, while in an actual game.

With my tiny hockey players, I have them begin by simply jumping over a hockey stick, as shown (Fig. 96), first from a standstill, then while moving slowly. Hopefully, they will learn at this point that the key to jumping is taking off with well-bent knees and landing with well-bent knees.

Next, I go on to the eight to twelve-year-olds and have them jump over two cones (Fig. 97) lying flat on the ice with a stick suspended across them. Make sure the cones are really lying flat, so that the stick is suspended only about 12 inches off the ice.

With my advanced hockey players I move on to jumping over two cones standing upright, with the stick suspended across them about 24 inches above the ice, as shown in Figure 98.

When I trained the Fort Worth Texans, an Islander farm team, I devised the following agility drill: have about twenty players form a circle all standing in the hockey position, with their sticks held tightly in both hands at waist level. The coach stands inside the circle, then skates *very* rapidly around the inside of the circle, holding the blade of a hockey stick sideways against the ice. The players jump rapidly over the stick as it sweeps around the circle. Next, the coach turns the toe of the stick blade to the ice, lifting the shaft up somewhat in the air, and again sweeps rapidly around the circle, while the players jump.

By the way, coaches, I recommend strongly that you wear a helmet when doing this drill. One night I was working with a Metropolitan League team of older, quite advanced boys. As I swept around the circle with my stick, one avid jumper came down so enthusiastically he crashed his stick on my bare head! Needless to

Figure 96

Figure 97

Figure 98

Figure 99: *Islanders Bob Bourne and Dave Lewis (in front) demonstrate the "slalom skate" under Barbara's watchful eye.*

say, I was carried off the ice in a complete fog. When I returned to teach the same group two weeks later, I wore a bright red hockey helmet, and was greeted with uproarious laughter when I skated onto the ice.

SLALOM SKATE

Many of the New York Islander players used to do this agility drill with me regularly. In Figure 99 you can see Islanders' Bobby Bourne and Dave Lewis weaving in and out of the cones much like skiers in slalom racing. This is another really good agility exercise, and not as easy as they make it look. Keep your head up, knees bent, stick close to the body for maneuverability.

Figure 100

Figure 101

Figure 102

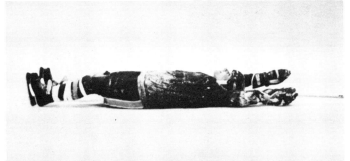

Figure 103

THREE-HUNDRED-SIXTY-DEGREE TURNS

In this agility drill the coach should have the group of skaters move rapidly down toward him/her, then at the sound of a whistle, the skaters execute complete 360-degree turns. This drill should be done with the skaters alternating the turns in both directions.

FORWARD SLIDE ROLLS

Skate rapidly down ice, then fall (Fig. 100), slide, and roll completely over onto your back (Fig. 101). Then roll back over to the side (Fig. 102), and get up again (Fig. 103). Most important of all, *get up fast*, and practice rolling over to both sides. Many hockey players in a fast-moving game will slide and roll over, but have difficulty getting up because they are confused and disoriented from the shock of the roll. This exercise will help them learn to take this kind of shock, while keeping their wits about them at the same time!

HOPS

Most coaches have players execute "hops" from a stationary position: the players simply line up facing the coach and at either a whistle or stick command, the players "hop" one foot over the other, in either direction to the side (Figs. 104 and 105). However, I recommend that the players be lined up one behind the other and begin skating rapidly around the outer perimeter of the ice, near the boards. When I give the signal, they "hop" to the side away from the boards (going toward the center of the rink), and at a second signal, they hop back toward the boards and resume skating when they are back in position next to the boards.

This "hop" is excellent not only for overall agility, but for perfecting takeoffs, and doing them while skat-

Figures 104 and 105: *like a row of
ballerinas, the players execute
"hops," an agility drill, crossing one
foot over the other first to one side,
then the other.*

ing instead of from a stationary position greatly increases skill.

SQUATS

The one-legged squat or "Shooting the Duck" exercise has already been discussed, but I often use the simple two-legged squat as an agility drill, to see how fast the player can get down and back up again. Forwards can occasionally use the squat to elude a defenseman, and it does work if done fast enough, but requires split-second timing.

I have the squat drills done in two ways. First, I have the players line up one in back of the other and then begin skating down ice, where they squat under a stick held by myself and coach Richie Hiller (Fig. 106). Other times I line the players up and have them begin skating, then every time I blow the whistle they squat and get up as fast as they can manage.

Figure 106

PUCK DRILLS

Up to this point I haven't once mentioned working with a puck, but I do have some agility drills for the players to do using the puck.

Have the players skate down ice, as rapidly as they can, while maneuvering the puck with their skate blades, as shown in Figure 107. I even have my skaters "shoot" the puck on the goal with one of their blades turned sideways. Forcefully remind them, of course, that shooting the puck in the net with their skates won't count in a real game—this drill is meant simply to develop agility with their feet, and is comparable to a soccer dribbling drill.

Really advanced players (for instance, I have done this with minor league professionals, and up to twenty of them at a time), can do what I call my "random stick-handling" exercise. I have the players skate with the stick and the puck, at random, between the blue lines of the rink. The object is to continue puck-handling and avoid the others the whole time.

After the players have done this for some time, I have them continue the same random puck-handling, but between the red line and the blue line. They then must work in a much smaller area, which requires greater skill and agility.

Remember, *heads up*. I have found that the average hockey player, even after years of skating and hockey playing, will stick-handle constantly with the head down.

Figure 107

SHOOTING

What I am about to describe now is truly an accuracy drill, but it requires great agility to perform. I have two boards made, one to cover each goalie net. Each has two notches cut into each upper corner, and a notch cut from the center of its bottom edge. Figure 108 shows all three notches.

The purpose of having my players shoot at these boards instead of at a live goalie is so that I can judge how agile and how accurate their shooting really is. It is always good experience for the skater to actually shoot at a goalie, and it's good for the goalie to get the practice, too. But often this gives the coach no detailed idea of the shooter's real abilities.

I have the players skate toward one goal, one at a time, and when they reach the blue line, I call out which notch I want them to shoot at, for instance, "left corner."

Figure 108: *the shooting board measures 6 feet wide by 4 feet high; the center slot is 2½ feet across by 7 inches high; and each corner net measures 12 inches by 12 inches. (Drawing by Gary Tinschert.)*

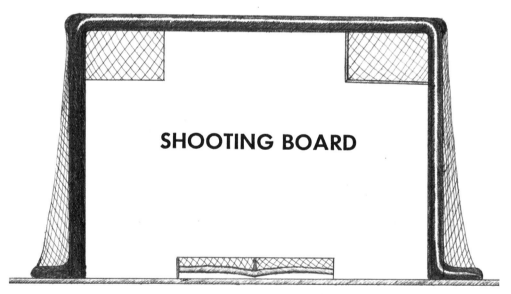

SHOOTING BOARD

POWER SKATING DRILLS

Now we come at last to the real meat of learning to skate with more power. It may have seemed a long way to get here, but until you have learned about the "good hockey position," have gotten a basic grasp of the concept of "edges" (most important), and have some idea of the need for conditioning, warm-ups, agility and balance drills, and the other things we've discussed earlier, you aren't really ready for power exercises and drills. Each drill is designed to strengthen a particular move essential to good skating in hockey. Many hockey players, including some pros, waste a lot of energy in executing their moves because they do not utilize the key to good, strong power skating. That is, they do not know how to make proper use of the *edges* of their blades. The correct use of the blades' edges is the secret to more power in your skating.

Again, always remember to start all of these exercises and drills slowly, gradually increasing your speed and the number of times you perform each drill. I have found that the best way to learn these drills is to do only two or three of them at each session, in the order in which I present them, and then repeat them each time thereafter on ice, adding another exercise or two, depending on the level of expertise of the skaters.

In the following drills we will refer to "forward" and "back" edges. Don't get confused: these terms do not refer to the "front" or "back" of your blades (which would take you off the balls of your feet), but instead refer to the direction in which the drills are done. For instance, the drill called "Forward Inside Edges" means that you will skate in the forward direction on your inside edges.

Most of the drills have names I have coined myself. They are, in many cases, virtually the same drills per-

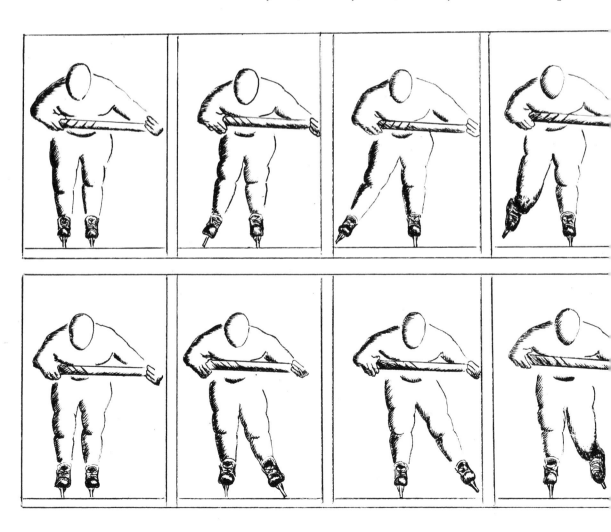

formed by figure skaters, only adapted for hockey, but I have also tried to make the names describe the movements executed as aptly as possible.

A note to goalies: the day when the worst skater on a pick-up team was automatically goalie is long over. Today's net-minding chores require excellent reflexes, speed, balance, agility, and maneuverability. Goalies always do any and all of these power drills in my class.

THE LONG EXERCISE

As you must have realized by this time, good skating, like any other skill (physical or mental), is largely a matter of constantly repeating and reviewing the correct moves. So, as we start our power drills, we always begin by getting into the good hockey position (see right-hand drawing in Figure 109).

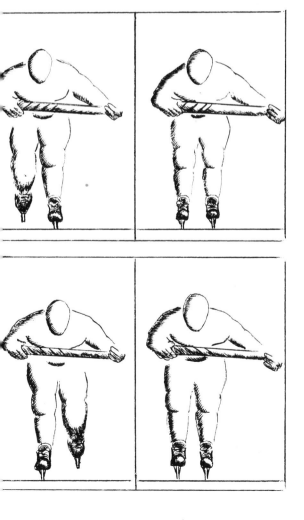

Figure 109: *top left, thrusting with the right foot. Bottom left, thrusting with the left foot. Above, good hockey position. (Drawings by Gary Tinschert.)*

Now, push off (or thrust) with either skate, to the side, keeping the weight on the ball of the foot. Extend the leg to its fullest, the skate close to the ice at the end of thrust, then bring the skate back to its original position, executing a half circle or letter "C" backwards and then, bringing the foot forward, glide for the count of two. (Figure 109 shows pushing first with the right, and then with the left foot.) The feet should be shoulder width apart during the glide.

Sounds like simplicity itself, right? Wrong. There are certain very important pitfalls to watch out for. Hockey players should always attempt to achieve a low center of gravity for increased stability and thrust. So, keep the *legs well bent* throughout the "Long Exercise," and do not move the torso from the hips up. Remember, skating takes place from the hips down, while hockey is played from the hips up!

Notice that I stressed extending the leg to the *side* with the weight on the *ball* of the foot. This is because it feels at first as though you should thrust to the back and put your weight on the toe. But resist this temptation, or you will end up running down the ice rather than skating. And if you don't thrust to the side, really digging into that inside edge, you will simply be skimming the surface of the ice and there will be no power (or ultimately, speed) to your skating.

THE STRIDE

Once the "Long Exercise" has been thoroughly learned and practiced—with all the don'ts completely erased —we are ready to work on the "Stride." This is basically the same as the previous drill, except that we do not glide for the count of two between thrusts, but instead push off with the other skate immediately.

Since we now have learned that we thrust to the side, with weight balanced, knees bent, upper torso stationary and head up, there is basically only one major point

Figure 110: *(Drawing by Gary Tinschert.)*

to remember when switching to the stride. And this is, that it is impossible to begin the thrust with one foot unless *both* feet are initially on the ice.

Again, this sounds extremely simple, but that is exactly the spot where trouble begins! The tendency with many hockey players is to shift weight virtually in the air, before returning the skate back to the starting point. This will have you "running" down the ice once again, rather than skating, and will take all the power out of the thrust.

So, when a thrust is finished, *make sure the weight is shifted completely to the returned foot before beginning the next thrust.* Figure 110 (A) shows the *wrong* procedure for shifting weight while skating; drawings (B) and (C) show the proper weight shifts.

Notice in (B) the player has already pushed off and now is bringing his right foot back to complete the stride. In (C) you can see the player has completed the stride and both feet are next to each other on the ice; the left foot is now ready to push off for the next thrust. Now, looking at (A) you can see that the player is virtually stepping with his right foot in the air and not bringing his feet together as they should be, as shown in (C). This bad habit creates the situation in

Figure 111

which the hockey player runs down the ice, rather than thrusting or skating.

At this point, the skater should be drilling with the hockey stick, and it is very important that the stick move properly with the weight shift on each thrust. For instance, when pushing off with the left foot, the right shoulder, knee, *and the stick* should be aligned over the right foot. Not only should the stick move in the direction of the weight shift, but it should move parallel or slightly downward (see Fig. 111) rather than up. Too many players tend to "wave" the stick too high, rather than simply move it. This is not only dangerous, but will contribute to improper upper torso movement.

If you find that you are having difficulty with stick and upper torso movement, there are three helpful exercises to practice which will aid in restricting upper body movement (Figs. 112–114).

FORWARD INSIDE EDGES—TWO FEET

After the "Long Exercise" and the "Stride" our next drill looks superficially as though we are going back to simpler exercises, but in fact, you will find it is difficult to execute this drill properly. This drill is an excellent one for strengthening the calf muscles.

Hold the hockey stick in front of you, at shoulder height. Bend your knees well, keep your head up and make sure your feet are underneath you, shoulder width apart, as shown in Figure 115. Remember that the feet are never raised from the ice when executing this drill.

Now, turn your toes out, and you will be pressing on your *inside* edges, as shown in Figures 116 and 117. Then, turn your toes in, your skates completing semi-circles (Fig. 118), and after "toeing in," *snap* your feet back into their original position, making sure you apply your weight to the back of your skates without lifting the blades. This "snap" is impossible to illustrate with still photographs, so be sure to push hard; you should hear a loud scraping noise from the skate blades as your feet return to the starting position.

The initial tendency of the skater when executing this drill will be to bounce up and down like a Yo-Yo as the blades snap back. Don't move at all from your hips, and the pressure will be properly applied to the whole

Figures 112–114: *skating with the arms locked (FIG. 112), with the stick held in front (FIG. 113), or with the stick in back (FIG. 114) will help the player learn to restrict upper torso movement.*

Figure 112

Figure 113

Figure 114

Figure 115   Figure 116

Figures 115–118: *holding the stick at shoulder height and keeping the feet on the ice at all times, the skater executes the* Forward Inside Edges, *Two Feet Drill: toes out on* inside *edges, then toes in and "snap" the feet together.*

skate blade rather than just to the front. Also, if your knees are properly bent throughout the drill, it will be impossible for you to "bounce."

FORWARD HALF INSIDE EDGES

This drill is basically the same as the previous one,

Figure 119   Figure 120   Figure 121

except that the skater thrusts, or turns, on one blade at a time rather than with both blades simultaneously. Remember to keep the whole blade on ice at all times, and do the drill with a short, quick thrust and a snap return. For greater stability, keep the foot which is not thrusting on a slight inside edge. Try not to sway from side to side with the upper torso too much, and try to aim straight forward (Figs. 119–123).

Figures 119–123: the Forward Half Inside Edges *Drill differs from the previous drill in that the skater thrusts or turns on one blade at a time, using a short, quick thrust and the "snap" return.*

Figure 124

Figure 125

Figure 126

FORWARD INSIDE EDGES—ONE FOOT

Unlike the two previous exercises, this drill is performed on one foot, rather than keeping both feet "glued" to the ice as in the two previous drills. Get in a good hockey position, then skate two or three strides. At command, push off with the *right inside* edge (Figs. 124 and 125). Now quickly raise the right foot slightly and "attach" it to the left skating foot (Fig. 126). The "attached" foot gives the player a better sensation of bal-

Figure 127

Figure 128

Figure 129

ance and stability. Notice that the right shoulder is slightly back, and the body executes a semicircle. The drill is then repeated, thrusting with the right foot, after returning the feet to their original position.

FORWARD OUTSIDE EDGES—ONE FOOT

Study the illustrations for this drill carefully (Figs. 127 —132), and read the explanation several times, if necessary, because I find that young skaters—and experienced hockey players—have a great deal of difficulty performing drills on outside edges.

Get into a good hockey position, then skate down the ice for two or three strides. At the command, lift your right skate slightly (Fig. 127). Cross it in front of your left skate, placing the blade down on the *right outside* edge, making sure your right shoulder is slightly forward (Fig. 128), and then thrust with the *left back outside* edge (Fig. 129). You will form an outside semicircle if you complete this drill correctly. This is a continuous drill, which means that you bring the left foot forward after the thrust (Fig 130), cross it over the right (Fig. 131), on the *left outside* edge, while thrusting with the *right back outside* edge (Fig. 132).

re 130   Figure 131   Figure 132

Figure 133

Figure 134

Figure 135

Figure 137

Figure 138

Figure 139

Figure 141

Figure 142

Figure 143

It is important to note that this drill is often performed in youth hockey by asking the skater to lift his/her foot up very high while crossing over. I disagree heartily with this tendency. Logically, if the foot is kept close to the ice, better balance can be maintained and the foot can be lowered all the more rapidly for the next thrust. There is no reason to raise the feet high on any power skating drill—it simply decreases efficiency. The matter may be further confused by the fact that many youngsters play football and hockey simultaneously, and their football coaches stress picking the feet up high, so that the poor youngsters pick the habit up there, too!

e 136

re 140

FORWARD COMBINATION OF EDGES—
INSIDE TO OUTSIDE

Skate down the ice and, at the signal, place your weight on your *right inside* edge (Fig. 133) and do a semicircle (with the left shoulder slightly back), as shown in Figure 134.

At the end of the semicircle, still on the same foot, shift your weight to your *right outside* edge (Fig. 135), creating an outside semicircle (with the left shoulder slightly forward). The left foot is "attached" to the right throughout this drill (Fig. 136). Notice that the slight shoulder movement follows the edges, but the torso should not jerk or bob. This drill will enable you to change from *inside* to *outside* edge rapidly, as in real game circumstances. Repeat the drill with the other foot.

THREE-HUNDRED-SIXTY-DEGREE TURNS

This exercise is performed while skating so rapidly down the ice that the player has no time to press on any edges and it is executed on the surface of the ice. Since the turn is done with such speed and virtually on the "flats" of the blades, it is difficult to describe, yet relatively easy to do. When I give the command to turn to the left, for instance, many skaters will press abruptly on a *right inside* edge, which will stop the turn!

For once it is easiest to describe a drill not by discussing edges, but by describing the upper torso's movements instead. Skate rapidly down the ice and upon command, simply ease your right shoulder forward, and your body and skates will follow. Both feet will then be under you on the "flats" of the blades, and you will execute a complete turn to the left. To execute the 360-degree turn in the other direction, ease your left shoulder slightly forward on command.

This drill is excellent for developing good balance, stability and recovery from a hard check.

MOHAWK TURNS

There are times, particularly in a defensive situation, when it is necessary to switch from skating forward to skating backward while moving in the same direction. This switch is called a Mohawk turn. In our example we will turn to the right.

The head turns first, along with the upper torso to the right, making sure that the hips move in unison with the shoulders. At this moment the left foot is on the *inside* edge, while the right foot is held back and slightly off the ice (Fig. 137). As you turn, the right foot is then placed down on an *inside* edge (Figs. 138 and 139), and you are now skating backward in the same direction (Fig. 140).

SKATING FROM BACKWARD TO FORWARD—SAME DIRECTION

As you look at the lengthy title for this drill, I am sure many of you wonder why this is not simply called a

"Reverse Mohawk." The reason is that while you will end up in the opposite direction, the moves you execute are different, and skating is very precise in describing its moves. So, this drill is not a Mohawk turn, but simply skating from backward to forward in the same direction. We will turn to the right in our example.

Skate backward down the ice (Fig. 141) and upon command, turn the head and upper torso to the right, placing the right foot forward on its *inside* edge (Fig. 142), while the left foot thrusts on its *inside* edge (Fig. 143). You are now skating forward in the same direction.

Now you can see why this is not simply a "Reverse Mohawk"; it is, in fact, simpler than a Mohawk turn, for by the time you complete the body motion, you are already skating in the other direction and thrusting.

FORWARD "BOSTON" OR "RINK" TURNS— ONE FOOT (OUTSIDE EDGES)

Skate down the ice, knees well bent with the head up, toward a cone placed on the ice. You will be skating to the left of the cone, making a turn to the right. At the cone, place your weight on your *right outside* edge, left shoulder forward and the left foot to the side, as shown (Figs. 144–146). Complete the drill by skating back in the direction from which you came.

For the turn on the *left outside* edge, skate toward the right side of the cone, place the weight on the *left outside* edge (Fig. 147), with the right shoulder forward, the right foot to the side (Fig. 148), then skate back in the same direction (Fig. 149).

FORWARD "BOSTON" OR "RINK" TURNS— ONE FOOT (INSIDE EDGES)

The drill differs slightly for inside edges. Skate toward the right of the cone. Place your weight on your *right*

Figure 144

Figure 145

Figure 146

Figure 147

Figure 148

Figure 149

inside edge (Fig. 150), with the left shoulder slightly back (Fig. 151) and the left foot "attached" to the right ankle, as shown (Fig. 152).

Next, skate to the left of the cone, and place the weight on the *left inside* edge when parallel with the cone (Fig. 153). The right shoulder should be slightly back (Fig. 154), with the right foot "attached" to the left ankle (Fig. 155). "Attaching" the leg will insure better balance.

re 150

Figure 151

Figure 152

re 153

Figure 154

Figure 155

FORWARD "BOSTON" OR "RINK" TURNS— TWO FEET

Skate toward the left side of the cone. When parallel with the cone, press the right shoulder back, placing the weight on the *right outside* edge (Fig. 156) while the left skate is on the *left inside* edge (Fig. 157), which stabilizes the turn to the right.

As with the previous rink turns, finish the drill by skating back in the direction from which you came and then repeat the drill with the other foot. Always make sure when doing this turn in actual games that you never "coast" or hold the turning position too long, as it will slow you down.

When reversing this drill, skate to the right of the cone, press the left shoulder back, your weight on your *left outside* edge while the turn is stabilized by your *right inside* edge.

Figure 156

Figure 157

Figure 158

Figure 159

"BOSTON" OR "RINK" TURNS—BLOCK POSITION

Skate toward the left side of the ubiquitous cone with the blades in the same position as the previous drill—*right outside* edge and *left inside* edge. However, press the right shoulder *forward* in a "blocking" or "screening" position, as shown in Figure 158.

If the cone were an opposition player, the right shoulder pressed forward instead of back would effectively block that player from the puck, hence the name of the drill.

Note that I have just told you to shift your shoulder contrary to the normal procedure, after telling you that the body will follow the turn. This is because by now, hopefully, you have learned to place your weight on your edges well enough so that you can, if the need arises, shift your shoulders contrary to the normal turn attitude, in order to block your opponent without losing speed or balance. A lot of players will ward off the opponent from the block position with their arms as well as their shoulders.

Figure 160: *to illustrate the Boston Turn, Block position, here is Barbara with Robby Benson, star of "Ice Castles." Note that Robby, whom I trained for the movie, is blocking me. He was an apt pupil. (Photo by Columbia Pictures/Paul Schumach.)*

Unfortunately, I have often observed that too many players—right up to NHL caliber—*always* perform their turns with their shoulders in the "block" position, even when there is no opponent nearby. This slows the turn considerably and makes it more difficult to execute. If there is no need to block, then don't! Instead, press your shoulder in the normal fashion.

To reverse the Boston Turn Two Feet Block Position, simply skate toward the cone's right side with your blades on the *left outside* edge and *right inside* edge, with the left shoulder forward in the block position, as shown in Figure 159.

I cannot stress strongly enough that when executing a turn in the block position you should always keep your head up—know where you're going or you'll simply be a dangerous menace on the ice! To yourself, as well as others (Fig. 160).

FORWARD INNER "SCOOTERS"

The name for this drill becomes apparent when you remember that a scooter is a toy on wheels that you *push with one foot* (actually, with today's mania for skateboards, I should probably call these "skateboards" —a skateboard is, after all, a sort of scooter without a handle!). Pushing with one foot is just what we're going to do, all in preparation for learning crossovers. All "scooters," backward or forward, are done in a circle.

Start in the hockey position, then press your left shoulder back. At the same time thrust to the side with the *right inside* edge (pressure on the ball of the foot), as far as your leg can extend, close to the ice (Fig. 161). Then return the right foot next to the left (Fig. 162), and pause for one count (Fig. 163). Now repeat the thrust with the *right inside* edge and return. The left foot, which is held on a *left outside* edge, does not move and the body performs an entire circle thrusting with the *right inside* edge. Do not bob the body up and down while thrusting.

To execute the inner scooter in reverse, press the right shoulder back, thrust to the side with the *left inside* edge, then return to the stationary right foot which remains on its *right inside* edge. Make sure you pause for that count between scooters, because I have found hockey players rush this drill. The pause is important to the *learning* of edges.

FORWARD OUTER "SCOOTERS"

From the good hockey position, press your left shoulder back. Instead of pushing with the *right inside* edge, thrust with the *right outside* edge, which is an extremely difficult maneuver, so look at the illustrations carefully.

| ure 161 | Figure 162 | Figure 163 |

Figure 164 Figure 165 Figure 166

Place the left foot into the inside of an imaginary circle (Fig. 164), then put pressure on the *left outside* edge and thrust that *left outside* edge behind the right foot, as shown (Figs. 165 and 166). Your right foot is held throughout on a *right inside* edge. When you return your left foot after the thrust (Fig. 167), place it back inside the circle, pause (Fig. 168), then repeat the drill moving in a large circle counterclockwise. To perform the drill clockwise, assume the good hockey position, right shoulder back. Place the right foot inside the circle with pressure on the *right outside* edge and

Figure 169 Figure 170

       Figure 168

thrust the *right outside* edge behind the left foot, holding the left foot on a *left inside* edge. Finally, return the right foot inside the circle after thrusting.

Now you are ready for continual crossovers.

FORWARD COMBINATION CROSSOVERS

Having mastered forward inside and outside scooters, you are now ready to combine them, which will give you a forward crossover. Begin this drill by working in a

      Figure 172   Figure 173

fairly large circle and, of course, get into the good hockey position.

We will be skating in a counterclockwise direction in this drill and the first step is to move your left shoulder slightly back (Fig. 169). Next, push off on a *right inside* edge as far as you can push, weight on the ball of the foot—not the toe, then release the foot (Fig. 170).

After completing this initial move, cross the right foot (close to the ice) over the left foot (Fig. 171), placing it on its *right inside* edge. At this moment the left foot is thrust behind the right foot, pushing hard on its *outside* edge (Fig. 172). After this thrust, the left foot is returned to its original position and you are ready to repeat the entire process over again (Fig. 173).

Hockey players often look as though they are running or hopping when they do crossovers. This is because they are wasting a terrific amount of energy by not using their edges properly. Always keep in mind that edges are the key to power skating, and unless you can dig them correctly into the ice you are merely skating on the surface, wasting energy and sacrificing stability and agility. Remember the crossover is not simply a maneuver, but also the most efficient technique for propelling the skater forward with strength, balance, and power.

In our society of virtually forced right-handedness, we have created skaters who find it extremely difficult to use the left foot with the same degree of proficiency as the right. One of the best results of learning to do crossovers well is overcoming this weakness of the left foot. But it takes a long, long time to correct this weakness and crossovers must be practiced diligently.

The forward crossover in the clockwise direction is simply a reversal of what we have done: lean your right shoulder slightly back, push off on a *left inside* edge, then release. Next, cross the left foot over the right, on its *inside* edge and thrust with the right foot on an *outside* edge.

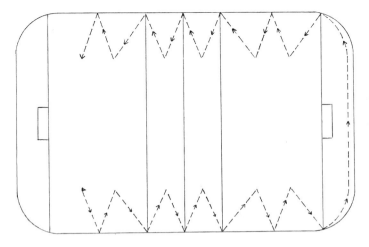

Figure 174: *this is the pattern a skater makes when doing "zig-zags" or alternating crossovers, rather than the circles executed when doing regular forward combination crossovers. This drill is important for learning actual game techniques. (Drawing by Gary Tinschert.)*

FORWARD ZIG-ZAGS

As a drill, forward crossovers are done in a circle. But in a game situation, an offensive player carrying the puck down ice will use forward crossovers in a zig-zag pattern done as follows.

The players skate forward rapidly and on command the right foot pushes on its *inside* edge, is picked up and placed in front of the left on its *inside* edge. The left foot is on an *outside* edge, and the left shoulder is back, as it thrusts behind the right.

Now, to zig-zag instead of moving in a circle, the players bring the right shoulder back as they move the left foot forward placing it very briefly parallel to the right foot. The left foot immediately pushes on an *inside* edge, is picked up, crossed over the right and is placed on its *inside* edge, while the right thrusts from behind on its *outside* edge. The players have just executed "alternating" crossovers, which moves them sideways in either direction rather than in the large circle, as Figure 174 indicates.

It is important that the skater remember to keep moving rapidly in this exercise. However, when attempting to perform the zig-zag rapidly, many players tend to forget the thrust of the crossover, and instead simply cross the feet. Again, remember that the crossover is a method of propelling the skate, and the thrust is equally as important as crossing over.

FORWARD CROSSOVERS—BLOCK POSITION

In this variation of the forward crossover, the edges on the right and left feet are identical to regular forward crossovers, as are the motions and the weight balance. The only change is in the shoulder position (See Fig. 160). In the counterclockwise direction the left shoulder is normally back, but since you want to block a player skating right next to you, bring your shoulder forward instead. In the clockwise direction, the right shoulder is forward rather than back. It may take a lot of practice to get these moves coordinated, but believe me, it will be worth every minute.

BACK-SKATING

One of the first derogatory remarks often made about a forward in professional hockey will invariably be, "He can't skate backwards." This is meant to be a reflection of the skater's lack of defensive abilities, since as a forward he plays a largely offensive role.

Unfortunately this comment is all too often true. Unfortunate because, in fact, there are many instances in which the forwards should cover for their defensemen. Therefore, the ability to skate backwards is an absolute essential. Much to my horror, there is such an emphasis placed on offense today, with the great increase in "offensive-defensemen" (thanks to the likes of Bobby Orr, Brad Park, and Denis Potvin who can score goals as well as any forward), that even young rearguard skaters are neglecting their back-skating. The following section on back-skating can solve this problem.

BACK INSIDE EDGES—TWO FEET

Assume our proverbial good hockey position with the hockey stick held in front at shoulder height. The feet

Figure 176   Figure 177

should be no more than shoulder width apart, nor should the feet leave the ice during this and the following drill.

Place your weight on the inside edges of your skates and "toe" both feet in, as indicated (Fig. 175). Your feet will thus complete two half circles (Fig. 176). As you return your skates to their original position, bring the heels together first (Fig. 177), then straighten the feet into their starting position.

A common tendency in this drill is to put too much pressure on the toes, causing the heels to come completely off the ice. This often results in a humiliating fall flat on the face! So, always keep your feet "glued" to the ice, making sure that pressure is applied evenly to the *ball* of the foot, even when "toeing" in.

BACK INSIDE HALF-EDGES

Get into the hockey position, with the exception of the stick. Hold the stick in one hand with the other hand close to the body as in Figure 178. Start with the *right inside back* edge. The right toe points in, to put the foot on the inside edge, executing a half circle (Fig. 179), then returns to its original position. Next, push with your *left back inside* edge (Fig. 180): left toe in, half

Figure 178   Figure 179

circle (Fig. 181), return. Please note that while you use one foot to perform the drill, the other foot is always on a light *inside* edge to lend stability while you thrust. This exercise is performed under real game situations by defensemen.

BACK "BOSTON" OR "RINK" TURN— ONE FOOT (OUTSIDE EDGE AND INSIDE SIDE)

These drills are identical to the body positions and edges for the forward "Boston" turns (see p. 122), except that you will be skating backward.

Figure 182   Figure 183   Figure 184

Figure 181

BACK INNER SCOOTERS

As in forward scooters, back scooters are always done in a circle. Once in the hockey position, place the left shoulder back, and look over your left shoulder (Fig. 182). You will be skating in a clockwise direction as you first take your right foot, toe it in (Fig. 183), and push on its *back inside* edge, making a half circle (Figs. 184 and 185). Again, keep the right foot on the ice at all times, even when you return it to its original position (Fig. 186).

While your right foot executes the half circle, the left

Figure 186

Figure 187: *at the end of a "thrust" I will sometimes ask a skater to raise the foot off the ice, just to see how he or she is balanced, although normally I say "never" raise the feet when doing back inner scooters.*

foot should be held stationary on a *back outside* edge. To perform the drill in a counterclockwise direction, just reverse the procedure: right shoulder back, look back over the right shoulder, toe in the left foot on a *back inside* edge, and keep the stationary (right) foot on a back outside edge. Execute the half circle and return.

These back scooters are excellent for developing good balance and stability in back-skating, as well as teaching the use of back inside edges, and they will prepare you for back crossovers.

Despite the fact that I have said never to lift your foot while peforming half circles in back-skating, *occasionally* I will ask a skater to hold up the "thrusting" foot to see how much balance has really been developed (Fig. 187).

BACK OUTER SCOOTERS

Having mastered the back scooters using inside edges you are now ready to tackle back outside scooters, and you will begin by taking the same position as in the previous drill: left shoulder back, look over left shoulder.

You will be skating in a clockwise direction as you place your left foot into a circle, virtually on the "flat" of its blade (Fig. 188), and then push hard toward the

Figure 188

Figure 189

edge of the circle (which puts that left foot on its out-side edge) in back of the right foot (Fig. 189). The right foot is on a *back inside* edge and does not move throughout the thrusting.

Be sure to push the left foot on its outside edge until you can push no further, then release the foot, lift it *slightly* and return it to the inside of the circle (Figs. 190 and 191).

When skating counterclockwise, reverse the proce-dure: hockey position, place right foot into circle on "flat," then push on outside edge as far as possible in back of left foot which is stationary on inside edge, release, raise right foot slightly and then return to in-side of circle.

BACKWARD COMBINATION CROSSOVERS

Now that you are ready to do back crossovers, I'd like to pause for a moment and remind you of something very important. I know, you have spent the last few drills perhaps feeling as though you have at least three left feet with no hope of ever figuring it all out! But re-member, it happens to every hockey player and they all manage to learn back-skating—at least to some extent. Once the strangeness passes (after much practice), it becomes second nature. You can console yourself with the image of Bobby Orr, Denis Potvin, and even Guy

Figure 190

Figure 191

Figure 192

Figure 193

Figure 194

Lafleur spending days and weeks doing the very same tedious and sometimes confusing drills.

Once you have mastered all of these power skating drills, you may still not end up a Guy Lafleur on the ice, but by golly, you're going to know what you're doing out there and you will be doing it well and confidently, so keep plugging—your spirits can help your skates as much as anything!

Having mastered both inside and outside back scooters, you are now going to combine them to perform the backward crossovers. These must be done in a large circle, and you will begin in the same hockey position as for the back scooters, first in a clockwise direction: place the left shoulder back and look over

Figure 196

Figure 197

Figure 195

your left shoulder.

Now, push with the *right back inside* edge. Next, lift the right foot (Fig. 192) over the left and place it on the ice on an *inside* edge. Make sure that when you push with the right foot, the left is on an *outside* edge. Now thrust the left foot, still on its *outside* edge, from behind the right foot (Fig. 193). When you can thrust no further, release the foot (Fig. 194), pick it up and return to the original position (Fig. 195), repeating this whole procedure several times until grasped.

To execute the drill in a counterclockwise direction, simply reverse the entire exercise: right shoulder back, look over the right shoulder, push with the left foot on its *back inside* edge, then lift the left foot over the right

Figure 198

Figure 199

Figure 200

(which is on an *outside* edge), thrust the right foot on its *outside* edge, behind the left. After full thrust, lift the right foot and return it to its original position.

BACK OUTSIDE EDGES—ONE FOOT

If you thought these previous back-skating exercises were difficult, you were wrong! Now we are going to get to the *really* hard part: using *back outside* edges. Most skaters seem to have much less difficulty, whether skating backward or forward, in grasping the concept and the feel of inside edges. The "feel" of outside edges is, well, strange and foreign at first and nearly all skaters have trouble learning to use outside edges. But study the illustrations carefully and practice hard— sooner or later the sense of that outside edge will come to you. The outside edge is essential to learning back crossovers, which are the defenseman's stock in trade for covering the opposition. This exercise is done in a straight line down the ice.

Get into the standard good hockey position and then begin skating backward. At the signal, lift the right foot (Fig. 196) over the left, making certain that the right heel crosses the left skate first. When you place the right skate on the ice, do so on its *outside*

Figure 201

Figure 202

Figure 203

edge (Fig. 197). At the precise moment you place that right skate on its *outside* edge, thrust the left skate backward on an *outside* edge also (Fig. 198). When you can thrust no further with the left foot, lift it slightly, and without touching the ice, bring it over the right foot (Fig. 199) and place it on its *outside* edge, while the right foot thrusts on its outside edge (Fig. 200). Continue this exercise down the length of the ice in a straight line.

BACK INSIDE EDGES—ONE FOOT

This drill is basically the same as forward inside edges, one foot (see p. 114), but is more difficult just because skating backward is harder to master.

Get into the standard good hockey position, then begin skating backward. At the signal, take the right skate and "toe in" slightly (Fig. 201), placing it on a *right back inside* edge, while "attaching" the left skate to the right (Fig. 202). The right foot will execute a half circle, after which the left foot is placed on the ice (Fig. 203), toed in on a *left back inside* edge, to execute the half circle. The right foot is "attached" to the left foot (Fig. 204). Continue this exercise down the ice in a straight line.

Figure 204

BACK CROSSOVERS—GOING DOWN ICE

The skater has now become accustomed to doing back crossovers, but has learned them in a large circle. This is the proper way to develop the skill, but doing crossovers in a large circle will not help a defenseman under actual game circumstances! It is necessary for a defenseman to skate backward, keep himself facing his oncoming opponent, yet skate from side to side simultaneously, covering his opponent's attempts to get around him.

From a good hockey position, the players start to skate forward. At the signal, they execute a Mohawk turn and skate backward, immediately beginning a back crossover: right skate pushes then crosses over left, while left thrusts back (see pp. 136–137, Figs. 192–195). However, at this point, instead of continuing to cross over leading with the right skate, the player pauses for a brief moment after the first crossover (on both *inside* edges, for balance)—as though he were sizing up his opponent's next move—then he does another crossover, but leads with the left skate, which will move him to the opposite side, while continuing to move backward at the same time. Thus, to move down ice (zig-zag rather than circle), the skater is doing "alternate" crossovers rather than "continuous" crossovers.

One night I was teaching back-skating to a class of six-year-olds who had been making really good progress. I decided it was time to do back crossovers going down ice. I explained to them that I wanted them to skate forward, do a Mohawk turn, then start backward doing crossovers, but to lead first with one foot, then with the other. Then I demonstrated to them what I expected.

The little ones were so excited to be finally doing something that real hockey players did, instead of some old drill, that they hardly paid any attention to my demonstration. When I blew the whistle they skated forward. I blew again and they neatly performed their Mohawks. But the minute they started doing their crossovers, I had twelve tiny players skating in circles! It was chaos. The poor tykes were so well-versed in doing back crossovers in a circle, they just couldn't break the habit. As I stood there holding my head in my hands, one stubborn little fellow stood in front of me saying, "But I *know* I can do back crossovers—*you* taught me."

So, coaches, explain what you want very carefully, then demonstrate the drill equally as carefully, and finally, let them try it. But, as soon as possible, divide the class into "defensemen" and "forwards" and simulate game circumstances. When they realize how important it is to keep their bodies facing those forwards, while at the same time moving backward and sideways, they'll really catch on to alternating the crossovers, down ice.

Two major faults often develop in doing back crossovers—whether it's down ice or in circles, and I see these two bad habits constantly in youth hockey. The first problem is that when a player executes a back crossover, he *slides* the lead foot over the thrusting foot instead of picking it up. Picking up the foot properly helps the skater to clarify his balance. When the lead skate is slid over, it is uncertain exactly where the weight will be shifted. However, when that foot is definitely picked up (not too high) and crossed over, it is clear that the weight will be on the back foot. Sliding the foot over is also much slower than picking it up crisply and crossing properly. As we all know, speed is too crucial in this game to waste time being lazy.

The second major fault is one in which a player sacrifices thrust for what he mistakenly thinks is speed, not thrusting properly in the crossover, as was pointed out earlier with forward zig-zags. Remember the movements: push with right back *inside* edge, then lift right foot over the left, placing it on its *inside* edge, *then thrust strongly with left foot, on its outside edge.* In the haste of a game, the skater may cross one foot over the other properly, but then forget to thrust with that back foot, cutting down the speed and power of his crossover.

STOPPING

Well, now you're skating up and down the ice backward and forward, but if you don't perfect this next series of drills, you are going to run into (literally) some serious complications on the ice. After all, what good does it do to get it all moving, if you can't stop it when you need to!

Whether you are a five-year-old "mite" or an NHL player, you must learn to "stop on a dime," because hockey is simply too fast-moving a game. And you must be able to stop and change directions rapidly throughout any of those fateful sixty minutes if it's required of you.

Many young hockey players—and some NHLers—I have trained have already perfected a fine sideways stop. Unfortunately, since all public skating rinks require only counterclockwise skating (left), they could only do it in one direction. The ability to stop only to one side can be a serious detriment to a player's game. Just as a player can become known for his inability to skate backward, it is also true that opposition players will ultimately spot the fact that another skater is weak

Figure 205: *forward snowplow stop.*

at stopping in one direction, and can take unmerciful advantage of that failing, leaving the hapless player watching their ice chips as they skate right around him!

FORWARD STOPS

So, here, we must go back to basics, in order to correct any weaknesses which may be already developed. The first stop to work on is the simple Forward SnowPlow Stop, skating down ice, as shown in Figure 205. Note the head and torso are held up, the knees well bent while pressure is being applied evenly to both *forward inside* edges. Practice this until you have eliminated any tendency to be on the toes of your skates, which will pitch you forward, with most uncomfortable results.

We next learn the Forward One Foot SnowPlow Stop. Skate down the ice with the knees well bent, then press the right foot slightly forward and apply pressure to the *inside* edge, as shown in Figure 206. The left foot remains on the ice on a slight inside edge for balance.

Figure 206: *forward one foot snowplow stop.*

Repeat the procedure with the left foot. Remember, if it's harder to do this stop with one foot—and nearly all of us are weaker with one foot than with the other—don't give up; just keep practicing with each foot.

The one foot snowplow stop is nearly always used by five to seven-year-old skaters in game play, because they can't master a full hockey stop.

Before we go on to the full hockey stop, we must first learn to stop on one foot, but not in the snowplow fashion. We will learn to do this with both the *inside* edges and the *outside* edges.

Figure 207 illustrates the One Foot Stop on the *right inside* edge. Skate rapidly down the ice and at the signal, turn the head to the left and bring the right shoulder forward. The right hip follows the shoulder immediately, and the right skate presses hard on its inside edge as it follows the hip. The left foot is lifted off the

Figure 207: *forward one foot stop,* inside *edge.*

Figure 208: *forward one foot stop, outside edge.*

ice and almost "attached" to the right. Repeat in *both* directions.

However, when we move to the One Foot Stop, Outside Edges, or T-Stop, we usually run into trouble again, because so few hockey players really have a good grasp of outside edges. In fact, this exercise usually ends up in disaster the first few times! Look closely at the illustration and read carefully.

Skate rapidly down the ice and at the signal, pick up the left skate slightly off the ice, and place it directly behind the right, but perpendicular to it, forming a "T" (Fig. 208). As the left foot is placed on the ice behind the right, it is on a *left outside* edge and the right foot is lifted immediately. The weight is over the left foot as the stop is completed.

If you find that you cannot grasp this maneuver, do the following: Drag the right foot on the ice (Fig. 209)

Figure 209

Figure 210

on an outside edge, until you come to a stop (Fig. 210); the left foot will remain on ice throughout. This way you will gradually begin to "feel" how to stop on an outside edge with one foot. This stop on the outside edge is used when leaving the ice and also by centers in the face-off circles, so you should master it.

We have now finally arrived at the Full Hockey Stop —the most important stop in hockey and one which *must* be learned in both directions (Fig. 211). The player skates at a high speed and on the signal turns the head left (direction of the turn). The right shoulder comes forward, with the right hip and skate following. As the right foot turns, it is pressed strongly on its *inside* edge while the left foot remains on the ice on an outside edge. The weight of the body is over the left foot at completion of the stop, which enables the skater to make a fast takeoff if necessary.

If the player were skating and stopped in front of the net, he would then be poised on both *inside* edges, as shown below. He is thus stabilized to prevent being knocked over by eager defenders (Fig. 212).

BACK STOPS

A defenseman must face the play of the game at all times, so it is logical that the Back SnowPlow Stop

Figure 211

Figure 212: *here is my son Tommy poised on his inside edges (for stability) as though waiting for a pass. (Photo by Kevin Rich.)*

Figure 213 Figure 214

would be the most often employed stop. It is the quickest way to stop backward and the player will never lose sight of the puck and the man he is covering. The player first skates backward rapidly, applying pressure to *both back inside* edges, thus stopping him, while the upper body is slightly pitched forward as in Figure 213.

I have found that few hockey players use this simple, quick, and effective back stop. Rather, they skate backward and then, when they have to stop, turn to their strong side, do a back hockey stop, then cross over and take off again. Unfortunately, this is a good way to lose sight of the puck and/or the man being covered, and it wastes time. Instead, master the One Foot Back Snow-Plow Stop which follows, and you will soon break the habit of the inappropriate back stop just described.

Skate backward rapidly and on signal apply pressure to the *left back inside* edge as Figure 214 shows. This will stop you, while you can still see the man you are checking—and the puck. The right foot remains on ice, forward (but close) to the left foot, on a slight *inside* edge. Always, always, ALWAYS master the stop with each foot.

Be sure to apply the pressure to the ball of whichever foot you are using to stop—not the toe—or you will stop abruptly with a great view of the ice at the end of your nose!

We have come to the Back Hockey Stop, which nine out of ten hockey players seem to use incessantly and unnecessarily because the back snowplow stop is certainly a faster way to stop. However, since it is used, it must be described properly: The player, skating backward rapidly, presses his right shoulder back, with the right hip and skate following. The right skate is on a deep inside edge; the left skate is on an outside edge; and the weight is over the left skate as the player stops.

While I prefer that defensemen not use a back hockey stop most of the time, if a player insists, I constantly remind him to keep his eyes on the play—not to turn his head away from the action when he presses his shoulder back. I must now confess to you that there *are* certain instances when a special variation of the back hockey stop is very useful. When defensemen are going into the corners, the sideways turn of the back hockey stop will give them excellent balance and stability when coming up against another player along the boards.

The player skates backward rapidly, then the right shoulder presses back along with the right hip and the right foot turns and presses on its *inside* edge as the left foot is also on an *inside* edge. The variation from the back hockey stop is that both feet are on *inside* edges. This is also the basic technique for a "hip check" on ice (Fig. 215). At this late date, do I have to remind you to practice this in both directions?

TAKEOFFS—FORWARD

Takeoffs are enormously important in actual hockey play, giving the skater great speed and power when performed correctly. Forward takeoffs are not nearly as

Figure 215: *Barbara and pupil Robby Benson, star of the movie "Ice Castles," are only pretending as she checks him into the boards, but note, nonetheless, that she has both feet on her inside edges, in the special variation of the back hockey stop. (Photo by Columbia Pictures/ Paul Schumach.)*

Figure 216

Figure 217

Figure 218

hard to learn as they are to describe, so observe the following illustrations and read carefully. I teach forward takeoffs in two steps.

Step One, get in position as though you have just completed a full hockey stop to the left: the right foot on an *inside* edge, while the left foot, bearing your weight, is on an *outside* edge. At the signal, apply pressure on the *right inside* edge to push off (Fig. 216), then "spring" the right skate over the left (Fig. 217), and finally, push the left skate off on an *outside* edge. I say "spring" rather than simply "cross" over because the right skate has first pushed into the ice and when it then moves over the left skate it springs or "vaults" over with the energy of that thrust.

Remember to keep your weight on the ball of the foot, not on the toes. This preliminary step to a complete forward takeoff should be performed several times in both directions and then we move on to Step Two.

Step Two, begin skating. At the signal, execute a full hockey stop to the left. However, without hesitating, do Step One just described (push on *right inside* edge, spring right foot over left, then push off with left skate on *outside* edge.) After Step One is executed, rotate the torso completely to the left (Fig. 218). You are now facing forward, but in the direction from which you just

Figure 219   Figure 220

skated. After the left foot finishes its thrust, it is brought forward and "dug in" on its forward *inside* edge, with the heel slightly off the ice. This "digging in" should be done for several steps—left, right, left—before moving into regular skating stride (Figs. 219 and 220).

After completing these steps to performing the forward takeoff, I like to have players develop the "dig" further. I divide the class into pairs, relatively equal in size and/or weight, if possible. The two skaters then place their hands on each other's shoulders in a hockey position. One player (the "resister") presses on his *inside* edges and resists being pushed down the ice. The other player (the "digger") "digs" his skates in and pushes the "resister" down the ice. It is virtually impossible for the "digger" to move the other skater, but the

Figure 221: *the "digger" (left) is attempting to push the "resister" down the ice.*

sensation of really digging the blades into the ice is experienced. In fact, everyone is usually panting with the effort of exertion at the end of the drill (Fig. 221).

Next, I tell the "resister" to ease up on his inside edges and let the "digger" move him. The frustrated digger will usually throw his heart into it this time—as well as his blades—and will move his partner down ice easily.

A note of caution: Often, in an excess of fervor, the skater doing a "dig" will end up on the toes of his skates with the heels far off the ice. No good. Raise the heels only slightly, keeping your weight on the balls of the foot, and remember to press on your forward *inside* edges (Fig. 222).

Figure 222: *here I am trying to "dig" while Islander forward Bob Nystrom plays the part of the "resister." Notice that my weight remains on the balls of my feet.*

TAKEOFFS—BACKWARD

While there is only one basic forward takeoff, there are three back takeoffs. The first is a takeoff from a back snowplow stop. Having completed the back snowplow stop, the player's upper torso will be projected slightly forward, which will give him a faster takeoff. Now, the player should "dig in" (as discussed in forward takeoffs, p. 151, Figs. 219 and 220). This digging-in motion with the forward parts of the blades should be done for two or three steps, after which the player goes right into his stride. This is, I feel, the quickest takeoff from skating backward.

When a player who has been skating backward makes a takeoff from a back hockey stop, he will have the right shoulder back, with the right hip and right skate under him. The right skate is on an *inside* edge. The left skate is on an *outside* edge, with the weight balanced over the skate.

Now the skater presses on his right *inside* edge, then springs his right skate over the left, placing it on an *inside* edge, and the left foot pushes on an *outside* edge, then comes forward and "digs." The "digs" should be repeated two or three times and then the skater goes into the stride. The player will now be skating forward in the direction from which he has just skated backward.

The takeoff from a back one foot snowplow stop is quite different from the two takeoffs we have just discussed. There will be no necessity to "dig" from a back one foot snowplow stop, and here's why.

When the player completes the back one foot snowplow stop, his left foot is on a deep *inside* edge, with the right foot slightly forward of the left, on a slight *inside* edge (Fig. 223). The left foot simply presses very hard on that inside edge, enabling the right foot to glide forward, and the player is already in stride (Fig. 224).

Figure 223

Figure 224

Figure 225

Figure 226

GOALIE DRILLS

At the end of my power skating sessions, I usually work with any goalies in the class on some special power drills which relate to their unique activities, having to do with speed, balance, agility, and blocking, not long distance skating moves. First take a look at the fully equipped goalie in his proper "defense" stance (Fig. 225).

The head is up but relaxed and the eyes should follow the puck, not the man, as many goalies mistakenly
do. Our goalie is wearing the "cage" mask preferred by
many professionals today because it offers complete
visibility, while the enclosed mask cuts visibility in the
corners of the eye holes and at the feet.

The goalie's torso is leaning slightly forward, but
were he to lean any further, he would be off-balance,
finding it difficult to breathe. The "catching" glove is
held with the palm facing out, while the stick is held on
the ice between the legs. The "waffle" mitt holding the
stick deflects pucks without injury.

The knees are well bent and touching, while the feet
are slightly apart. The stick is positioned to cover the
gap between the pads at ice level.

Side Slides

The goalie simply moves one skate to one side, then
glides the other next to it, keeping the feet on the ice
the whole time.

Side Thrusts

(Fig. 226). The goalie has skated out from the cage to
cut down the angle, and then wants to move rapidly to

Figure 227   Figure 228

Figure 229: *kick save.*

Figure 230

one side. He turns one skate in the direction he wishes to skate, then puts the other skate behind it in a "T" and thrusts.

Falling and Rising

(Figs. 227 and 228). Basically the same as knee drops, this should be done both from a stationary position, and while moving. It should also be done one-legged and then two-legged.

Kick Saves

(Fig. 229).

Stack the Pads

(Fig. 230). One form of "save," this is done both to the right and the left.

"Shimmy" Out and Back from the Net

(Fig. 231). In this drill the goalie "inches" out from the cage by moving with the feet held together. The pads are held together, too, as the feet execute a parallel pattern on the ice. This is not really a "swizzle" since the feet stay together, rather than moving separately (Fig. 231B).

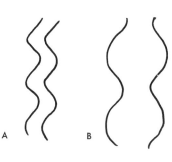

Figure 231 (A): goalie "shimmy" pattern with skates, unlike "swizzle" power drill (B). (Drawing by Gary Tinschert.)

Figure 232

Figure 233

Figure 234

Figure 235

Figure 236

Skating Around the Net
(Figs. 232–234).

Hops
(Figs. 235–238).

Glove/Stick Reflex Drill
The coach stands in front of the goalie who is in the net in the ready position. The coach calls either "stick" or "glove" at random, at which point the goalie rapidly maneuvers whichever is called, as though making arm, glove or stick saves. The key word is "rapidly," since this is a drill to develop speed reflexes.

Figures 232–234: *skating around the net.*

Figures 235–238: *hops.*

gure 237

Figure 238

Figure 239

Split Save

(Fig. 239). This is identical to the "splitz" warm-up exercise, but notice the glove and stick ready to deflect the puck.

Pads and Stick Save

(Fig. 240).

Figure 240: *pads and stick save.*

PROFESSIONAL INSIGHTS

When you have been around rinks for as many years as I have, both learning and teaching, you realize that there is a lot more to hockey than skates, pucks, and sticks—elements which are just as important to the life of the sport. There are a few things I'd like to add to these areas about coaches, rinks, senior hockey and women.

COACHES: TYRANTS OR FRIENDS?

When I first came in contact with youth hockey, I was shocked to learn that most of the coaches are parents of the boys in the programs. Even more shocking to me was the fact that many of them had hardly been on skates in their lives. I know that in little league baseball it is quite common for fathers to coach teams, and most of them have never been baseball pros. But here we are talking about hockey and skating, and good skating requires great skill to execute and to teach. Good skating cannot be taught by one who has never learned it thoroughly.

The result, all too often, is that children do learn to play a form of hockey, while never learning to skate properly. I recommend that training seminars be required for coaches involved in youth hockey. The Professional Skaters Guild of America (for figure skaters only) sponsors national seminars all year, as well as publishing a national newsletter—similar training could be instituted for youth hockey coaches. I feel that I am always learning my sport, skating, and I think that youth hockey coaches should realize that they, too, have a lot to learn.

The other striking thing about many youth hockey coaches is what can best be called the "macho" attitude. Coaches' macho behavior takes many forms, ranging from the constant screaming of obscenities at even young children, to demanding that all sessions result in working up a good "sweat," to refusing to allow the youngsters a drink of water during a workout. These points may sound trivial, but such "trivialities" can affect a youngster's whole attitude toward hockey.

As a parent and a skating coach, I "sit" on both sides of the boards at times, and I don't like to see someone swearing constantly at my kids. I realize that many a youth hockey coach has already put in a hard day's work at an office, and it is often difficult not to get short-tempered late at night with twenty-five excited, energetic youngsters. But that's what coaching is all about: patience (lots of it) and understanding. These players are not hardened pros or grown men; these are kids. They deserve respect and tolerance, just as the coach should be respected. Proving you know all the obscenities in the English language is no way to get respect, however. Proving that you know what you are talking about and teaching it well will always produce better results.

Coaches are not the only people I see yelling at the hapless kids, however. If I had a dollar for every parent (unfortunately, fathers, you are more often the culprits) I have seen screaming and raging at his or her child, I could own a minor league hockey team! This parental diatribe not only distracts the child, but usually upsets him, almost ruining his game.

And after the game, I usually would see that same child walking beside the enraged parent, head down (tail figuratively between the legs) and mute—all because of some momentary error.

One parent I remember in particular might help to clarify why screaming from the sidelines is so useless and potentially harmful. This father was continuously yelling at his son during games, correcting him loudly in front of everyone. Finally one night I had had enough of this parent. I skated over to him and asked him *loudly* how long his son had been skating. He blurted out something like . . . "four months."

I told him that there would be a father-son hockey game in a couple of months and that I would be happy to work with him, free of charge, once a week until the night of the game, and I did. The "big game" finally came and passed, whereupon the chagrined father walked, or I should say, crawled, over to me in front of the assembled parents and children, saying, "Gee, everything looks so easy and simple from the bleachers, but it's a h——— of a lot harder on the ice!"

From that night on the father still shouted occasionally, but it was encouragement and positive reinforcement to his son. Please, parents, identify with your child's positive attributes, not his or her failings.

As far as working up a sweat, well, I can't count how many times youth hockey coaches have skated up to me after a power skating session and asked me, "What kind of a workout was that—they're not even sweating!" Slowly and carefully I try to explain to them that there is much more to power skating than speed and wind sprints. Their expectation is part of that "macho" attitude again—unless the skaters are on the verge of collapse, drowning in sweat, they're not really "men."

Speaking of sweat, I'm sure you've heard the horror stories of young football players collapsing after a practice because of dehydration. And yet I find constantly that some youth hockey coaches won't allow water bottles at skating sessions. That's very silly—and dangerous. It's far better simply to explain to the kids that too much cold water while working out is unhealthy, and then let them take a sip occasionally during practices. Remember, all you "macho" types, most professional players take sips from a water bottle during regular games in all major sports.

Along the same line is the stubborn insistence of many coaches that their youngsters make hockey a year-round obsession. This is, I think, a serious mistake. The summer months should be spent doing other sports and physical activities. How does the old saying go: "Too much work makes Johnny a dull boy?" This is true of the hockey player who is involved with the sport all year—he will be dull, and more important, he will go very stale.

Ironically, the coach who wants his youngsters to make hockey an obsession will often be so obsessed himself, solely with competition and winning, that he practically ignores the kids who are not "first-line" or all-star caliber. This happens in other sports, too, but I wish the American Hockey Association would institute rules concerning "equal play time" for all youngsters whether it be an all-star team or a "house" league. And I don't understand why parents meekly tolerate such favoritism, considering the fact that they usually have shelled out hundreds of dollars in equipment and lessons, only to find that if their child doesn't qualify for the "first line," he or she barely gets to play.

There are times, though, when competition and incentive can be positive for the young player. Many coaches will not let a youngster play with the team if his or her academic average is not as least average, and I think that this qualification is healthy, adding incentive to the youngster's desire to "make the team."

The International Skaters Institute of America publishes a booklet entitled "Hockey Competition" which can be used by any coach at any rink. It suggests guidelines for team competition in timing and accuracy in passing, shooting, and skating.

One more small point about coaching. I find that most of them have skaters perform their drills between lines: from blue line to blue line, for instance. To improve their skaters' reflexes and responses, they would do much better to use a whistle for drills; then the skaters won't know when they will have to shift into the next motion, and will have to develop quickness.

I don't want to leave you with an entirely one-sided negative picture of youth hockey coaches, because I have worked with some of the finest out on Long Island —coaches who truly take an interest in the individual child, bringing out the best of each youngster on and off the ice, no matter how limited that child's abilities might be.

RINKS: JOIN THE TWENTIETH CENTURY!

American ice rinks *all* require counterclockwise skating. This means we have a world full of people who can only skate to their left! If you think about this for a moment, you'll realize how absurd it is. I have wasted hours and hours attempting to strengthen skaters preparing for the Olympics, as well as hockey and other figure skaters, in clockwise skating. Until recently a great many Canadian hockey skaters were brought up skating on ponds, and they learned to skate in any direction. It is time for American ice rinks to join the twentieth century, and add clockwise skating to their repertoire.

For future reference, coaches, I want to point out that the center of nearly all rinks is reserved for "free style" skating. I always remind rink owners of this fact when they protest having hockey skaters at mid-ice, and remind them that hockey skaters do "free style" maneuvers too. This will aid in breaking the counterclockwise-only experience of your players.

Another ploy which should be used more by hockey coaches is the "patch" session. This is a figure skating term for using an untouched corner of a rink for the skater to "etch" his moves on clean ice. I have even begun to use the "figure eight" drill with hockey skaters, and use "patch" sessions regularly in private lessons at several rinks.

SENIOR HOCKEY: IT'S NEVER TOO LATE

I have had less experience with senior men's hockey than with youth hockey, but I think it's important to mention. The more people we have actually participating in the sport of hockey, no matter how casually, the better it will be for the game.

My first senior men's class was a team made up of the New York City Fire Department! The first thing I decided to do was to give them all a "pep talk." So I stood up there and preached at them that they had to get their bodies in shape to play hockey, which meant no smoking, no beer or other alcoholic beverages, and no late hours. At the end of my sermon, all of them skated right off the ice!

After we all had had our laugh, I put them through their first workout, which I am sure they thought would be a breeze. One of them later described what it had been like when he said that he felt "as though he had been out all night fighting the worst possible fire." But these fellows personified what senior men's hockey is all about. They came out there to work hard, after working all day, doing it late at night, too.

One of my former senior men's hockey students, Larry Cangro, has put a lot of thought into the problems of senior hockey, and I'd like to share them with you. Larry, by the way, didn't start playing hockey, or taking power skating lessons, until he was thirty-six years old, recommended to me by his daughter, to whom I was teaching figure skating. Larry has also run the gamut of senior leagues—ones below his team's level, others way above his head, and teams which had very young men mixed in with oldsters (his team was once beaten 23-0!).

Larry begins by advising the novice senior to buy his equipment from a professional and take skating lessons, which of course is good advice. Further, he advises:

> After you are reasonably confident in your skating ability, start playing in a beginners, "no check" league. Ask questions regarding the fairness of how teams are selected, and state your own qualifications honestly. If possible, watch a few games first, to see how well you will fit in with the team.
>
> Don't move up until you have at least six months' experience. You might even be better off if you don't move up at all—I had more fun at this level than higher up the ladder.
>
> Keep your objectives realistic: exercise and fun.
>
> Don't be overly concerned about injuries. Anything can happen in any sport, especially one played on a slippery surface, but I have never seen anything more serious than a pulled muscle to anyone wearing proper equipment.

Larry goes on to make some very intelligent suggestions which rinks would be well advised to follow with regard to senior hockey. Larry would like to see rinks provide two professional coaches for all senior hockey games, and adult clinics on skills and strategy.

Cangro also pleads for more consideration in scheduling senior hockey games. Most ice time for such contests is offered very late at night (11:00 P.M. to 1:00 A.M.) which is terribly hard on older people who have already worked a full day, and have to get up early to go back to work.

Finally, my "senior hockey expert" would like to see much more effort put into screening skills for the different senior divisions, particularly on the lower levels—so that a player will have a better opportunity to play within his own degree of skill. This would include dividing the seniors into age groups. As Larry points out:

"Adolescents are divided into four or five age groups for very obvious reasons. Why is it not as obvious that a thirty-eight-year-old man cannot be expected to keep up with someone twenty years his junior?"

AND WOMEN, TOO!

If you take a long, hard look at all the various hockey papers and magazines, you will notice an almost complete dearth of articles concerning women and hockey. This will have to change soon, because women are entering the game more and more. In fact, many colleges, especially in the East and northern Midwest, are now offering women's hockey teams.

Women usually play a non-checking game, but they wear the full protective equipment. That's right, equipment made especially for the female anatomy has been available for some time now, so, women, don't let someone talk you out of the game because the equipment isn't designed for you.

There are a couple of important "lacks" in women's hockey at the moment, however. There are few qualified coaches for women's hockey; most women's leagues, except for colleges, mix tykes with adults; and hockey scholarships for women are still a dream of the future. Hopefully change will come soon for women's hockey.

One thing I would not like to see soon, though, especially in adult hockey, is women playing with men. They have learned in youth sports that there is little difference between the immature female and male bodies, and the two sexes are beginning to mix. But if women were allowed to play with men as adults, I think they would never be able to develop their skills in their own way—they would always be behind the men. Until there is equal time, money, and talent spent on women's hockey, there is no way they can be equals of the men.

To a fine young man
and a dedicated and gifted hockey player

RANDY BOY

Faces change and seasons pass,
Life goes on but nothing lasts forever,
The sun it shines, you got it made
In your prime, can heaven wait—no never.
You can think of me, but cry for me just awhile,
'cause when you think of me,
I'd love to be seeing your smile.

People I can feel praying,
People try to hear me saying,
I'm gonna see you again.

Don't ask the reasons why,
You'll never find words to satisfy,
Just find your comfort in
I'm gonna see you again.

Randy Boy, skating to the "Comfort Inn"
Mommy and Daddy's pride and joy,
Your memory is going to live forever.